A PRINCIPAL'S GUIDE TO LITERACY INSTRUCTION

TOOLS FOR TEACHING LITERACY

Donna Ogle and Camille Blachowicz, Series Editors

This highly practical series includes two kinds of books: (1) grade-specific titles for first-time teachers or those teaching a particular grade for the first time; (2) books on key literacy topics that cut across all grades, such as integrating literacy with technology and science, teaching literacy through the arts, and fluency. Written by outstanding educators who know what works based on extensive classroom experience, each research-based volume features hands-on activities, reproducibles, and best practices for promoting student achievement. These books are also suitable as texts for undergraduate- or graduate-level courses; preservice teachers will find them informative and accessible.

TEACHING LITERACY IN SIXTH GRADE
Karen Wood and Maryann Mraz

TEACHING LITERACY IN KINDERGARTEN
Lea M. McGee and Lesley Mandel Morrow

INTEGRATING INSTRUCTION: LITERACY AND SCIENCE
Judy McKee and Donna Ogle

TEACHING LITERACY IN SECOND GRADE
Jeanne R. Paratore and Rachel L. McCormack

TEACHING LITERACY IN FIRST GRADE
Diane Lapp, James Flood, Kelly Moore, and Maria Nichols

PARTNERING FOR FLUENCY
Mary Kay Moskal and Camille Blachowicz

TEACHING LITERACY THROUGH THE ARTS
Nan L. McDonald and Douglas Fisher

TEACHING LITERACY IN FIFTH GRADE
Susan I. McMahon and Jacqueline Wells

TEACHING LITERACY IN THIRD GRADE
Janice F. Almasi, Keli Garas-York, and Leigh-Ann Hildreth

INTEGRATING LITERACY AND TECHNOLOGY:
EFFECTIVE PRACTICE FOR GRADES K–6
Susan Watts Taffe and Carolyn B. Gwinn

DEVELOPING LITERACY IN PRESCHOOL
Lesley Mandel Morrow

TEACHING LITERACY IN FOURTH GRADE
Denise Johnson

INTEGRATING LITERACY AND MATH: STRATEGIES FOR K–6 TEACHERS
Ellen Fogelberg, Carole Skalinder, Patti Satz, Barbara Hiller, Lisa Bernstein, and Sandra Vitantonio

A PRINCIPAL'S GUIDE TO LITERACY INSTRUCTION
Carol S. Beers, James W. Beers, and Jeffrey O. Smith

TEACHING ENGLISH LANGUAGE LEARNERS:
LITERACY STRATEGIES AND RESOURCES FOR K–6
Shelley Hong Xu

A PRINCIPAL'S GUIDE TO LITERACY INSTRUCTION

Carol S. Beers
James W. Beers
Jeffrey O. Smith

Series Editors' Note by Donna Ogle and Camille Blachowicz

THE GUILFORD PRESS
New York London

A Division of Guilford Publications, Inc.
72 Spring Street, New York, NY 10012
www.guilford.com

Printed in the United States of America

This book is printed on acid-free paper.

Last digit is print number: 9 8 7 6 5 4 3 2 1

Library of Congress Cataloging-in-Publication Data

Beers, Carol S.
A principal's guide to literacy instruction / Carol S. Beers, James W. Beers, and Jeffrey O. Smith.
p. cm. — (Tools for teaching literacy)
Includes bibliographical references and index.
ISBN 978-1-60623-472-3 (pbk.: alk. paper) — ISBN 978-1-60623-473-0 (hardcover: alk. paper)
1. Literacy. 2. Interdisciplinary approach in education. 3. General education. I. Beers, James W., 1946– II. Smith, Jeffrey O. III. Title.
LC149.B44 2010
372.6′044—dc22

2009037566

ABOUT THE AUTHORS

Carol S. Beers, EdD, is Executive Professor in the School of Education at the College of William and Mary in Williamsburg, Virginia. She has held a variety of positions in education during her career, including that of classroom teacher, principal, reading supervisor, assistant superintendent, superintendent, and tenured professor. Dr. Beers has consulted nationally and internationally, presented frequently, and published widely. She has served in several capacities with the International Reading Association, including representing the organization on the National Joint Council for Learning Disabilities and serving on the National Commission for Diverse Learners, the Reading and Writing for Critical Thinking (RWCT) project, and the Manuscript and Policy Review Board. Dr. Beers has received Fulbright Awards for study in Japan and Germany, a Blue Ribbon Award for her work as a principal, an Honor Award from the National Association of Elementary School Principals, and several research awards from universities at which she taught.

James W. Beers, PhD, is Professor of Reading, Language, and Literacy in the School of Education at the College of William and Mary. He is also Director of the Eastern Virginia Writing Project of the National Writing Project, which trains teachers to help their students become better writers. Dr. Beers has taught reading, writing, and spelling to students at all grade levels and has published books, chapters, and articles on reading, writing, and spelling, among these *Developmental and Cognitive Aspects of Learning to Spell* and *Writing for Competency.* He is also an author of *Scott Foresman Language Arts, Scott Foresman Reading,* and *Scott Foresman Spelling.* He recently coauthored (with Donna Ogle) a college language arts textbook, *Engaging the Language Arts: Exploring the Power of Language.*

Jeffrey O. Smith, EdD, is Division Superintendent in West Point, Virginia, a school district that continues to be recognized for the students' high academic achievement. He has worked as a classroom teacher, assistant principal, and principal, and as an assistant superintendent in the area of instructional services. Dr. Smith's combined experiences have provided him with the opportunity to work as an instructional leader in rural, suburban, and urban educational settings from 1,500 to 32,000 students. Additionally, he has served as Adjunct Professor at Old Dominion University. He has received numerous honors and has been featured at the state and national levels for his students' achievements, his community leadership, and his work as an educator. In 1988, Dr. Smith was recognized as one of "ten achievers" in a special edition of *Ebony* magazine entitled "Save the Children!"

SERIES EDITORS' NOTE

This is an exciting time to be involved in literacy education. Across the United States, thoughtful practitioners and teacher educators are developing and fine-tuning their instructional practices to maximize learning opportunities for children. These cutting-edge practices deserve to be shared more broadly. Because of these changes, we have become aware of the need for a series of books for thoughtful practitioners who want a practical, research-based overview of current topics in literacy instruction. We also collaborate with staff developers and study group directors who want effective inservice materials that they can use with professionals and colleagues at many different levels that provide specific insights about literacy instruction. Thus the Tools for Teaching Literacy series was created.

This series would not be complete without this book for the building principal. For teachers to grow and provide excellent literacy instruction, they need the leadership and support of knowledgeable administrators. Everyone in the school is more likely to be on the same page when they can share resources like this Tools for Teaching Literacy series. With this book for principals, the entire professional team can study literacy together.

We thank Carol S. Beers, James W. Beers, and Jeffrey O. Smith for sharing their many years of experience as school leaders. Each chapter is replete with current information about what is needed to create quality literacy programs. The key principles of good instruction are outlined in the first chapter. Then the authors propose ideas for establishing a literacy-rich culture in the school, for creating ongoing professional development, and for helping teachers engage in self-assessment with their literacy portfolios. The ways in which building principals can collaborate with school literacy teams, reading specialists, and coaches are highlighted too.

Schools function best when there is a commonality of purpose and the teachers and administrators continue to learn together. This book provides support for schools that want to be even more effective in their literacy efforts. We hope both principals and the instructional staff will find ideas for discussion within its contents. Enjoy reading and discussing the chapters. Try several of the suggestions. Good teachers deserve well-informed and competent principals. Good principals deserve open and engaged teachers.

DONNA OGLE
CAMILLE BLACHOWICZ

PREFACE

How do principals deal with the complexity of their jobs and still serve as instructional leaders in their schools? The increased pressure of national and state standards has placed additional demands on principals' shoulders, making the issue of instructional leadership even more compelling. The task may seem overwhelming at times. This book is intended to serve as a guide for elementary principals who want to be literacy leaders in their schools. Each chapter addresses key elements of literacy leadership and provides specific suggestions to assist principals in their quest to be strong leaders.

The chapters of this book provide a practical guide on literacy leadership for elementary principals. Each chapter focuses on an element believed essential for strong literacy leadership and is organized around these key elements. Chapter 1 introduces the components of good literacy instruction (as identified by the National Reading Panel). Chapter 2 focuses on how to establish a strong literacy culture within a school. Chapter 3 explains how to initiate an elementary school professional development program that sustains strong literacy practices among staff. Chapter 4 addresses the challenges of literacy assessment and describes appropriate literacy assessment techniques to use with students. Involving families in partnership with schools is the focus of Chapter 5. Chapter 6, the final chapter, presents ways to assess the strengths and needs of elementary school teachers with respect to literacy instructional strategies. Each chapter contains lots of examples of student work and/or the work of staff members to illustrate ways that other schools have approached the topic at hand.

All of us are seasoned veterans of school leadership teams. Three of the authors (and the contributing author of Chapter 3) have had extensive experience as principals, one (C.S.B.) as the principal of a blue-ribbon school recognized for its strong literacy practices and culture. Two of us (C.S.B. and J.O.S.) also have district-level leadership experience in a variety of settings, which brings a unique perspective to the challenges of literacy leadership. One of us (J.W.B.) is a reading and writing educator at the college level and has worked with principals and teachers in high-need school districts for over 30 years. Our experience makes the book a practical resource guide for elementary principals who truly want to help their teachers help their students become better readers and writers.

CONTENTS

A PRINCIPAL'S GUIDE TO LITERACY INSTRUCTION

CHAPTER 1

WHAT MAKES GOOD LITERACY INSTRUCTION?

> All genuine learning is active, not passive. It involves the use of the mind, not just the memory. It is a process of discovery in which the student is the main agent, not the teacher.
>
> —ADLER (1982)

As educators, we live in an era of accountability unlike any other. On the national level, there has been a continual push to develop accountability measures, not the least of which include national tests. On the state level, there are increasingly higher and more complex accountability measures that drive schools and school districts. On the local level, parents and community members continue to push for reforms to ensure children have access to the highest level of education possible. Even the business community has entered the picture, with their focus on developing more students who have the soft skills as well as the technical skills to enter the workplace.

In 2001, No Child Left Behind (NCLB) legislation was enacted for the nation. The intent of this legislation was to ensure that schools and school districts focused on every child's achievement as they designed instructional programs. For the first time, states were required to disaggregate data and report how children were achieving in reading, writing, math, science, and social studies. Because of this initiative, school report cards were initiated and distributed to the public at large. As a result, parents and community members could now access data that allowed them to compare schools within a district as well as across the state. This type of scrutiny was a new phenomenon for many educators.

In addition to NCLB, the Reading First initiatives (2001) provided financial resources to states to ensure that proven methods of early reading instruction were present in classrooms. Through Reading First, local school districts receive support to ensure that all children learn to read well by the end of third grade. The funds were restricted to "research-based practices" in the hopes of initiating a more systematic approach to beginning reading instruction. This initiative reflected the Department of Education's attempt to force the issue of more phonics instruction in the early years.

The NCLB legislation, coupled with the Reading First initiative, has placed a greater demand for accountability on schools and their principals than ever before. Principals not only must have an awareness of their literacy program, they also must provide leadership in the building to ensure that their literacy program is consistent with best practices and current research. At the same time, they must keep staff focused "on the prize," which is helping all children become literate. Principals are, indeed, key players in this new accountability system. In order to provide grounded leadership, principals must understand the best practices in literacy instruction. These practices are focused on six key principles:

1. Literacy development proceeds through predictable developmental stages.
2. Good literacy instruction is balanced.
3. Good literacy instruction occurs across all curricular areas.
4. Reading and writing for meaning cannot be overemphasized.
5. Discussion and other oral language strategies are critical.
6. Diversity should be celebrated in classrooms and across the school.

LITERACY DEVELOPMENT PROCEEDS THROUGH PREDICTABLE DEVELOPMENTAL STAGES

The foundations for reading are laid long before students enter school. During the preschool years, children are learning about how their language system works, developing their vocabularies, learning something about stories and story grammar, and learning something about print. This foundation is built on rich and varied experiences, meaningful conversations, and exposure to a variety of stories and books. These years prepare children for their early school literacy experiences.

Throughout this process, children progress through stages (or phases) as they learn to read and write. These stages are not discrete stages, but rather overlap. Understanding the stages of development can provide staff with guidance in choosing the best instructional strategies to meet the needs of a particular group of students.

Chall's Model of Reading Stages

Chall (1983) first described stages of reading progress more than 25 years ago. Chall's stages made distinctions between "learning to read" and "reading to learn." These stages were not uniformly accepted at the time, primarily because of a controversy about whether children learn to read without comprehension. Nevertheless, there is a sense today that these stages provide meaningful insight into students' literacy development.

Stage 0

This is an early reading or emergent literacy stage, which Chall refers to as a *prereading* stage. During this stage, the child develops a foundation for reading instruction. For example, children become more adept with the sounds of their language system, with a growing awareness of what sounds are similar in words. Children develop concepts about print (e.g., print goes from left to right and top to bottom), phonemic awareness, and knowledge about how to handle a book. They also recognize that print is important, as it represents the actual words being told in the story. Generally, this is a stage seen in *preschool and kindergarten*.

Stage 1

This stage reflects the beginning of formal reading instruction and is referred to as the *decoding* stage. In this stage, children begin to develop some basic letter–sound correspondences and begin to apply this knowledge to books and other text. Children generally achieve an understanding of the alphabetic principle and should be given ample opportunities to "decode" words during this stage. Typically, children reach this stage in the *first grade*, between ages 6 and 7.

Stage 2

In Stage 2, children confirm the knowledge they learned in the prior stages and become more fluent with these skills. They develop what is referred to as automaticity, or the automatic reading of words, with less emphasis on decoding. As their reading becomes more fluent, they start to develop the ability to read in ways that reflect natural conversational rhythms (or prosody). They know how to use appropriate phrasing, stress, and intonation in their reading. Once children can do this, it is much easier for them to understand what they are reading. Chall refers to this stage as the *confirmation* stage and notes that is usually reached in *grades 2 to 3*, or around the age of 8.

Stage 3

This *reading-to-learn* stage points to a shift in motivation, with children starting to read to gain information. During this stage, they are typically exposed to more nonfiction (or expository) texts. Much of this material is presented in their science and social studies classes. This stage is usually achieved in the *fourth through eighth grade*, between the ages of 9 and 13.

Stage 4

During this stage, children are able to deal with a variety of viewpoints on a given topic through exposure to a variety of sources on a subject. Chall refers to these *multiple viewpoints* as essential in developing mature readers, because it is through these viewpoints that children begin to learn how to read critically and evaluate the information from the sources. Children in *high school* (between the ages of 14 and 19) are generally working through this stage.

Stage 5

Chall's final stage involves the ability to synthesize a variety of viewpoints. Through this synthesis, students develop their own perspectives on a subject, a skill that is necessary for critical reading. Chall terms the stage *construction and judgment,* as it is during this stage that students construct knowledge from what others have written and form opinions. Chall notes that this stage is after high school, generally in *college.*

Chall's model emphasizes that children need to focus on automatically decoding words once they have developed a basic knowledge of letter–sound correspondence. Without such automatic processing, students will spend a large amount of their energy and attention on the act of decoding, which leaves them with an inadequate amount of energy and time for comprehension (Adams, 1990). In other words, automaticity is necessary if learners are to succeed at the primary purpose of reading, the construction of meaning from text

Other Models

Ogle and Beers (2008) have presented literacy benchmarks in an easy-to-understand table. These benchmarks, which are an adaptation of Cooper and Kiger's (2005), are comprehensive, primarily because they include writing and spelling, in addition to reading. Table 1.1 summarizes these literacy benchmarks, which school staff members may find useful.

Vogt and Shearer (2007) argue that it may be helpful to view stages and/or phases as a continuum that is loosely woven. Ogle and Beers (2009) emphasize that development in various stages often overlaps, which demonstrates the need to view development as a continuous process, not a discrete one. This approach may help provide perspective, so that children are recognized as individuals who may have different paths in their reading journey.

TABLE 1.1. Language Arts Development Benchmarks

Early emergent literacy preschool)

- Oral language
  1. Begins to use different language functions
  2. Listens to and enjoys stories
  3. Enjoys rhyming and other word play
  4. Knowledge of grammar and language conventions grows
- Reading
  1. Acquiring print concepts
  2. Knows purpose of print
  3. Knows familiar writing genres
  4. Predicts and constructs meaning
  5. Retells familiar story
  6. Enjoys listening to literature read aloud
  7. Has beginning phonemic awareness
- Writing
  1. Knows what writing is for
  2. Tries to write or pretends to write
  3. Learning left to right progression
  4. Uses variety of writing implements
  5. Asks what something says
- Spelling
  1. Knows some letters
  2. Knows sounds of some letters
  3. Begins to be aware of letter–sound links
  4. Writes letters and letter-like forms

Emergent literacy (grades K–1)

- Oral Language
  1. Uses standard sentence construction
  2. Participates in discussions
  3. Has facility with oral language
- Reading
  1. Knows most print concepts
  2. Can track written words spoken aloud in text
  3. Learning common phonic elements in words
  4. Matches upper- and lowercase letters
  5. Has growing phonemic awareness
  6. Able to use story elements in retelling

(continued)

TABLE 1.1. *(continued)*

- Writing
  1. Uses letters in writing and uses other writing conventions
  2. Knows all letters of the alphabet
  3. Uses invented spelling in writing
  4. Writes in journals and shares writing
  5. Beginning to add story and informational writing to personal writing
  6. Starting to use the writing process

- Spelling
  1. Represents beginning and ending sounds in words
  2. Spells some words correctly
  3. Moving toward complete phonetic spelling of words

Beginning reading and writing (grades 1–2 or 3)

- Oral language
  1. Use of standard English grows
  2. Uses language in a variety of settings
  3. Interest in words grows

- Reading
  1. Sight vocabulary continues to grow
  2. Reading fluency grows
  3. Uses phonics and structural analysis for word recognition
  4. Uses context to learn words and their meanings
  5. Uses variety of comprehension strategies
  6. Has positive attitude about reading
  7. Begins to used text resources in all subjects

- Writing
  1. Demonstrates widespread writing
  2. Shares writing
  3. Writes in different genres for different purposes
  4. Uses the writing process
  5. Gains control over writing conventions

- Spelling
  1. Spells more words correctly
  2. Recognizes common spelling patterns
  3. Becomes aware of features to spell words besides letter-sounds

(continued)

TABLE 1.1. *(continued)*

Almost fluent reading and writing (grades 2–4 or 5)

- Oral language
  1. Continues to increase use of standard English
  2. Learning to differentiate between standard and nonstandard English
  3. Increases use of all language functions
  4. Increases speaking and listening vocabulary
  5. Aware of language techniques used by speakers
- Reading
  1. Uses all word recognition strategies
  2. Has instructional reading level at least at grade level
  3. Continues to increase use of comprehension strategies
  4. Enjoys reading independently in different genres for different purposes
  5. Silent reading grows
  6. Developing research skills through variety of media and texts
- Writing
  1. Writes for different purposes and audiences
  2. Uses different writing forms and genres
  3. Self-evaluates writing
  4. Shares writing
  5. Uses feedback in revision
  6. Grows in knowledge and use of writing conventions
  7. Makes links between reading and writing
- Spelling
  1. Grows in knowledge of spelling patterns
  2. Makes link between spelling, pronunciation, and structural elements in words
  3. Edits for spelling effectively
  4. Increases percentage of words spelled correctly in writing

Fluent reading and writing (grades 5–12)

- Oral language
  1. Uses language in a variety of functions
  2. Uses language with a variety of audiences
  3. Moves between formal an informal modes of talking
  4. Vocabulary continues to grow
- Reading
  1. Adjusts reading to meet purpose for reading
  2. Understands and reads different genres
  3. Uses a variety of comprehension strategies
  4. Enjoys reading
  5. Expands research skills

(continued)

TABLE 1.1. *(continued)*

- Writing
  1. Continues to expand purposes for writing
  2. Uses writing rubrics and self-evaluation to assess writing
  3. Uses writing process
  4. Uses different techniques for prewriting and revising
  5. Demonstrates voice and style in writing
  6. Continues to make connections between reading and writing different genres
- Spelling
  1. Widely uses conventional spelling
  2. Edits for spelling correctly
  3. Makes spelling connections among alternate forms of words
  4. Adds meaning to pronunciation and structural elements as guide to spelling

Note. From Ogle and Beers (2009, adapted from Cooper & Kiger, 2005). Copyright 2009 by Allyn & Bacon. Reprinted by permission.

Stages help us better understand the instructional needs of children. Children do not move lock-step through these stages, and their progress through these stages often varies significantly. By viewing these stages flexibly, however, they do provide us with insight into children's progress. A flexible perspective will also help us avoid labeling children as "at-risk" or "poor readers" too early in their school careers.

GOOD LITERACY INSTRUCTION IS BALANCED

We no longer live and teach during a time when we can be blind proponents of one method of teaching reading and literacy to students. There is simply too much research from the last decade that provides insight into how students learn literacy skills. That is why there is such emphasis on "balanced literacy" instruction in today's classrooms. What exactly does the term *balanced literacy* mean?

Balanced literacy merges the ideas of whole language and skills-based instruction. The National Reading Panel (2000) noted that the best literacy instruction incorporates strategic comprehension skills and automatic word recognition skills. Teachers who practice balanced literacy realize that some students require more support, while other students may need different strategies. These teachers integrate word study with active comprehension strategies in their classrooms. In the classroom, an observer would note both whole-class and small-group instruction. This instruction takes place in an environment that is rich with authentic children's literature and has meaningful opportunities for reading and writing. In many ways, a classroom that uses a balanced approach might look like a whole language classroom, but with explicit skills instruction included.

Those educators who are proponents of balanced literacy programs do not get caught up in either whole language or phonics debates. They recognize the value of both approaches. They use whole language because they believe that their students will become stronger readers if they are immersed in texts rich with interesting characters and story plots. They incorporate meaningful response to literature because they want their students to be engaged in literacy, not bystanders of it. They also incorporate explicit skills instruction into their classrooms, which are already filled with meaningful literacy practices. This skills instruction takes place in the following areas:

- Phonemic awareness
- Word recognition
- Fluency
- Vocabulary
- Comprehension

The amount of time that should be spent in each of these areas may differ depending on the grade level of students. Instruction in phonemic awareness, for example, might be more important in kindergarten classrooms than in fifth-grade classrooms. Similarly, emphasizing fluency in reading might be more important in first grade than it is in fifth grade. On the other hand, making sure that children are cognitively aware of the reading strategies they use as they try to understand a science text may have more emphasis in the upper elementary grades than in first grade.

Phonemic Awareness in Kindergarten and First-Grade Classrooms

Phonemic awareness is the understanding that spoken words are made up of sounds. This awareness develops gradually as children have experiences with word play, nursery rhymes, and stories. The work of the National Reading Panel (2000) found that instruction in phonemic awareness is a good predictor of later reading achievement and includes focusing attention on the phonemes in syllables and words. This same panel reached the conclusion that phonemic awareness instruction is effective in promoting early reading and writing skills, especially in kindergarten and first grade. Adams's work (1990) suggests that there are five stages of phonemic awareness:

- Recognizing rhyming words
- Detecting words that are the same or different in a set of words
- Blending sounds to make words
- Segmenting a one-syllable word into its sounds
- Identifying the word left when phonemes are removed or added

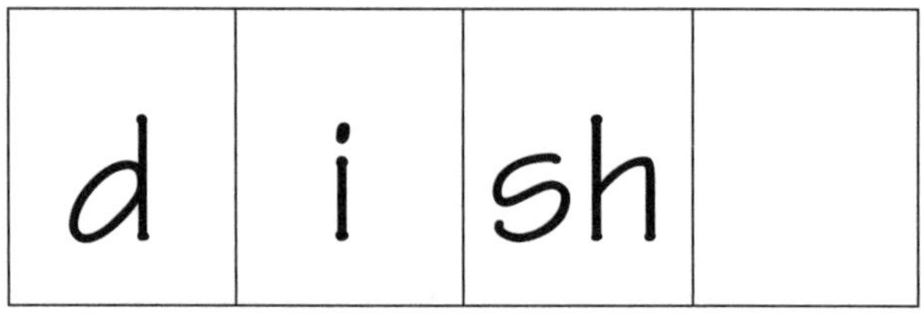

FIGURE 1.1. Sample sound box.

In order to develop phonemic awareness in children, teachers should provide a wide array of activities, including reading nursery rhymes and poems, making up simple rhymes with children, playing games with rhyming words, doing finger plays, clapping the number of syllables heard in words, and helping children to identify the similarities in sounds of different words. In addition to these activities, words sorts, sound boxes, and games can be especially helpful. Figure 1.1 gives an example of sound boxes. Sound boxes help students hear and record the sounds in order. In Figure 1.1, the word *dish* is segmented into three sounds and recorded in three of the four boxes provided.

RESOURCES

Principals can promote the use of phonemic awareness training in the primary grades by providing resources to teachers. One excellent resource emphasizes the use of the word sorts mentioned above: *Words Their Way: Word Study for Phonics, Vocabulary, and Spelling Instruction* (Bear, Invernizzi, Templeton, Johnston, 2008). A second resource is *Words Sorts and More: Sound, Pattern, and Meaning Explorations K–3* (Ganske, 2006).

Word Recognition Skills Should Be Incorporated into Reading Lessons

In order for students to learn to read, they must be taught how to recognize words. There are several ways this instruction can occur, but two approaches that are substantiated by a great deal of research include phonics instruction and teaching "word families" (or teaching by analogies). Phonics is the study of the relationship between the written letters in a word and the spoken sound that is heard. There is substantial evidence that phonics knowledge is a strong predictor of reading proficiency (National Reading Panel, 2000).

Word-recognition knowledge grows gradually during the early school years. Ehri's phases of sight word development help us understand the phases children go through. Ehri (1995) focused on the beginning stages of word recognition. Through her research, she determined that children go through four distinct phases as they learn how to read words automatically.

1. During the *prealphabetic* phase, beginning readers remember words by using visual cues (e.g., the word *look* has two "eyes" in the middle). Letter–sound relationships are generally not involved in the recognition process during this phase, thus it is called the prealphabetic phase. This strategy becomes insufficient as children develop a larger repertoire of sight words.

2. The second phase includes *partial alphabetic* recognition. Children in this phase recognize some of the letters and their corresponding sounds–usually the initial or final consonants. Using the initial and final consonant sounds is an important step, but an incomplete strategy.

3. As children continue to refine their knowledge of letter–sound correspondences, they develop more complete *alphabetic coding*. Children in this phase know how most letters represent sounds in conventional spelling. Thus, they can recognize different words with similar spellings, such as *mat*, *mate*, and *mart*. This ability helps them read new words. Words that they encounter frequently become sight words, thus allowing more immediate recognition.

4. The *consolidated alphabetic* phase is the final phase of automatic word recognition. During this phase, children learn to recognize letter patterns as units, thereby chunking bigger units as they read. This ability makes it easier for them to learn new words more quickly, thus increasing their ability to comprehend more difficult text.

Teaching Phonics

As mentioned earlier, phonics is a method of teaching word recognition that relies on the relationship of letters and letter groups to the sounds they represent. One assumption of phonics instruction recognizes that most languages have consistent letter–sound relationships. Another assumption of phonics instruction is that once children learn these letter–sound relationships, they will be able to pronounce the written words in their language system. Phonics instruction is generally considered to be helpful as children move through the stages identified by Ehri.

There are two different approaches to teaching phonics: analytic phonics and synthetic phonics. In the analytic approach (sometimes referred to as 'intrinsic' phonics), there are a variety of texts that children might use: their language experience stories, their predictable pattern books, a basal reader, or even a good story book. The teacher using this approach presents words that a child might know and then asks children to analyze the word by examining its letter–sound relationships: "You know the word *cat* begins with the *k* sound. Do you know some other words in our story that begin with this *c* sound?" Many teachers use this approach very successfully.

In a synthetic phonics approach, children's first texts have been written to carefully reflect their decoding skills. Often, the texts (called decodable text) is restricted to the sounds they have learned, plus some sight words they may know.

In contrast to the analytic approach, the synthetic approach presents the letter–sound relationship and then asks children to blend those sounds into words. "You know the sound of *c*, the sound of *a*, and the sound of *t*. Let's put them all together to make a new word." Many teachers also successfully use the synthetic approach to teaching phonics. Table 1.2 outlines the major differences between analytic and synthetic phonics.

While several researchers have argued the best way to teach phonics, there seems to be no distinct advantage to one method of teaching phonics over the other (National Reading Panel, 2000). This same report from the National Reading Panel did present persuasive evidence, however, that phonics should be taught *systematically* rather than incidentally. In systematic phonics instruction, there is a sequential set of phonic elements that are taught explicitly, whether through analytic or synthetic phonics. This is in contrast to many practices today, in which letters and sounds are introduced in an incidental manner with no planned sequence for instruction to guide teachers. Systematic phonics instruction provides children with one tool for recognizing words and has been found to be especially effective with struggling readers.

TABLE 1.2. Analytic versus Synthetic Phonics

Analytic phonics	Synthetic phonics
Teacher puts sentence on board with key word in it: *The boy fed his cat.*	Teacher puts word family on board and introduces the sound it makes: *at.*
Teacher puts other words on board that have same phonic element (*c): *cake, can, cap.*	Teacher introduces words that have *at* sound in them*: cat, rat, and pat.*
Phonic element is never separated from the word. Students observe that the words begin with the same sound.	Phonic element is emphasized separately from the word. Students are asked to say the sound of the individual letter out loud.
Auditory discrimination exercises are provided by asking children to identify which other words begin like the *c* in *cat*: *dog, car, boy, cop.*	New words are generated by using word families along with different phonic element: *bat, sat, mat, fat, and cat.*
Practice is provided with new words to see if children can blend the new sound to make new words: Last—cast; Pup—cup; Lot—cot.	Nonsense combinations may be encouraged, since they might reflect patterns in words they will meet later: *bat—batter.*
Finally, children are asked to read sentences in context: *I gave my cat a pat.*	Practice is provided in highly controlled text, even if the sentence does not make sense.

Teaching Analogies

Another way to develop word recognition skills is through the use of analogies. In this approach, children learn unknown words by looking for a familiar pattern that they already know in other words. Children then use this pattern to decode the unknown word. For example, the student who knows the word *rain* can be taught to use the word chunk *ain* to make several new words, such as *main*, *train*, *vain*, and *gain*. Pressley's research (2006) suggests that once a child knows the letters and sounds, the use of analogies can help them move to a higher level of word recognition.

The use of analogies helps students focus on word chunks rather than individual letters and sounds. This "chunking" is thought to be a more mature strategy, as students who continue to focus on individual letters and sounds expend a great deal of effort decoding, with little energy left for comprehension. Some even suggest that this chunking strategy should be used with young children, as these children can use onsets and rimes (i.e., spelling patterns). A primary way of teaching these words parts, or chunks, is through word families, or spelling patterns that are common to many words (see Table 1.3).

Teaching Instant Word Recognition

While a great deal of discussion at a national level has focused on teaching phonics, it is also important to realize that children must begin to recognize words instantaneously if they are to become fluent and mature readers. Mature readers do not sound out every word, but rather instantly recognize words and their meanings in texts. That instant recognition is referred to as a "sight vocabulary" and is important for children to develop. Instant recognition leads to automatic responses to text. This automaticity is considered critical for effective reading comprehension (National Reading Panel, 2000). Sight vocabulary develops as children repeatedly see the same words in a variety of contexts. While this may seem a daunting task,

TABLE 1.3. Some Common Spelling Patterns

ack	*ank*	*eat*	*ill*	*ock*
ail	*ap*	*ell*	*in*	*oke*
ain	*ash*	*est*	*ine*	*op*
ake	*at*	*ice*	*ing*	*ore*
ale	*ate*	*ick*	*ink*	*ot*
ame	*aw*	*ide*	*ip*	*uck*
an	*ay*	*ight*	*it*	*ug*
ump	*unk*			

there are researchers who have found that 500 words account for 90 percent of the running words in children's text (Cooper & Pikulski, 2000).

There are several approaches to developing this instant recognition, including repeated readings, word games (such as Bingo and Concentration), as well as word sorts and word walls. The value of these games is that students see and use words over and over, thus building their automatic recognition of them.

RESOURCES

One resource which principals can provide is *Phonics They Use: Words for Reading and Writing* (Cunningham, 2005). Another resource that will help teachers understand teaching word recognition by analogies is *Success with Struggling Readers: The Benchmark School Approach* (Gaskins, 2005). Finally, a resource for developing automaticity is *Partnering for Fluency* (Moskal & Blachowicz, 2006).

Developing Fluency Plays an Important Role in the Early Grades

Fluency is thought to be a critical factor in reading comprehension, primarily because fluent readers can read with accuracy, expression, and appropriate speed. Students who do not read fluently often falter over words and struggle to make sentences sound right. Students who do not read fluently are often so focused on individual words that they cannot recall the beginnings of sentences or paragraphs. These students often have comprehension difficulties.

Students who can read fluently are not "word-bound" but focus on larger chunks of meaningful text as they read. Fluency is closely related to the automaticity mentioned earlier, although it is not the same. The Rand Research Report (Snow, 2002) noted that early instruction in fluency ensures that older readers can focus more on comprehension as they read. The National Reading Panel (2000) found evidence that guided oral reading was most effective in developing fluency. Pressley (2006) cites the effectiveness of repeated readings. Research is not clear, however, about how much emphasis should be placed on fluency.

Repeated Reading

How does a teacher go about providing the opportunity for repeated readings? There are a variety of ways this can be done.

Students should engage in a lot of guided oral reading with books at their independent level. This means that they can read the text with about 95% accuracy, misreading only 1 out of 20 words. This independent level allows them to focus less on word recognition and more on fluency.

In the early grades, teachers may read the same book more than once. Teachers may also have familiar books available to students in the book corner, so that children have the opportunity to practice reading a familiar book more than once.

The importance of this type of repeated reading may be seen in Reading Recovery, where teachers use repeated reading as a strategy in each lesson.

Repeated reading is a useful strategy for children who are having difficulties. In these cases, the instructor selects a passage that is about 100 to 200 words long. The student is asked to read the passage. If the student misreads a word or hesitates, he or she is asked to read the word aloud and to repeat the word. Once the student has read the passage, the teacher asks the student to read the passage again, for a total of about four readings. Research (Rasinsky, 1990) has demonstrated that this strategy is highly effective for struggling readers.

Other strategies that make use of guided oral reading include choral reading, student–adult reading, peer reading, tape-assisted reading, and Readers' Theatre.

Choral Reading

In choral reading, children read as a group with the teacher or other adult. Because choral reading is usually done with big books, children typically follow along as the teacher reads from a big book. Books that have predictable patterns are good for choral reading, because children enjoy the style and want to join in. The letter in Figure 1.2 reflects a child's enjoyment at reading *The Old Woman and The Rice Thief*, a story with a highly predictable pattern.

Dear Dr. Beers,
Thank you for reading The Old Woman and the Rice Thief. I liked the story. The mouse was the funniest. The mouse was my favorite character. I can add the book to my collection of favorite books.
Your friend,
Samantha

FIGURE 1.2. Student letter.

Student–Adult Reading

In student–adult reading, the student reads one-on-one with an adult. The adult can be anyone: a teacher, a parent, a classroom aide, or a tutor. The adult reads the text first, providing the student with a model of fluent reading. Then the student reads the same passage to the adult with the adult providing assistance and encouragement. The student rereads the passage until the reading is quite fluent. This should take approximately three to four readings.

Peer Reading

There are variations to peer reading. During peer reading, students take turns reading aloud to each other. Sometimes more fluent readers are paired with less fluent readers. Sometimes children at the same level are paired to practice reading a story that the teacher has modeled for them.

Tape-Assisted Reading

During tape-assisted reading, students read their books while listening to a tape recording of the book; preferably the books are at the student's independent level. With the first reading, students follow along, pointing to each word as it is said on the tape. In subsequent readings, students try to read aloud along with the tape.

Readers' Theatre

In Readers' Theatre, children perform a play by reading from scripts that have been derived from the books they have read. Students assume the roles of characters or a narrator. Readers' Theatre is often used to give students a legitimate reason to reread text and practice fluency.

RESOURCES

Principals may want to consider purchasing *Partnering for Fluency* (Moskal & Blachowicz, 2006), mentioned earlier in this chapter. This text has many ideas to encourage more fluent reading in the classroom.

Strong Vocabulary Instruction Should Emphasize Integration, Repetition, and Meaningful Use

A balanced literacy program should emphasize the development of strong vocabularies in students, as vocabulary development is thought to be important for reading comprehension. The National Reading Panel (2000) concluded that vocabulary should be taught through direct and indirect strategies. There is some research that suggests that children who read only 10 minutes a day have a higher rate of vocabulary growth than those who do not. So, an important caveat about vocabulary: time should be set aside each day for reading stories and books.

Beck, McKeown, and Kucan (2002) present a framework for vocabulary instruction that identifies three tiers of words. Tier One words are basic words that rarely require attention in school but are used frequently, such as *baby, walk,* and *run*. Tier Two words are found across a variety of content areas but are not highly specialized, such as *laborious*, *fortunate*, and *coincidental*. Tier Three words are low-frequency words that are discipline specific, such as *peninsula*, *cumulus*, and *refinery*. Beck and her colleagues estimate that about 8,000 basic words (Tier One words) need no instruction, and they emphasize that instruction should focus on Tier Two and Tier Three words.

Nagy (1988) suggests several important principles for effective vocabulary instructions: integration, repetition, and meaningful use. *Integration* refers to the notion that vocabulary instruction should integrate the new words with prior knowledge. There are many strategies that illustrate this integration, including semantic mapping, Venn diagrams, and picture walks. The connect two activity shown in Figure 1.3 shows how children can integrate new words with those already known. During this activity, children connect words in their story in ways they choose, and present their rationale for the connections they have made. The teacher records these connections in a diagram.

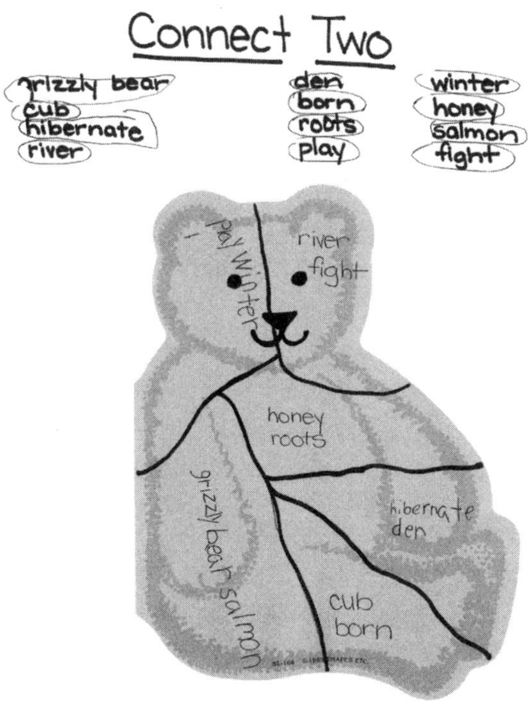

FIGURE 1.3. Connect two.

The second principle, *repetition*, ensures that students will be able to access the meaning of a word quickly and easily, without struggling. Nagy suggests that the best way to provide for this repetition is through *meaningful use*. In other words, in order for vocabulary instruction to be effective, students must have the opportunity to use the vocabulary in their reading and writing. Teachers can provide these opportunities through structured activities and games, but also through selected reading and writing materials. The probable passages activity (Figures 1.4 and 1.5) shows how a student was able to use new vocabulary from a story in a meaningful writing activity. In this particular passage, the teacher introduced the vocabulary words on cards and asked the student to place them in groups according to story features: character, setting, problem, and solution. After the student did this, a story frame was used to help the student write a prediction about the story. Subsequent to the story frame, the student wrote his own summary of the story.

Blachowicz and Fisher (2006) build further on the notion of meaningful use by suggesting four principles to guide vocabulary instruction, mainly that students should:

- Be active in developing their understanding of words.
- Personalize vocabulary learning.

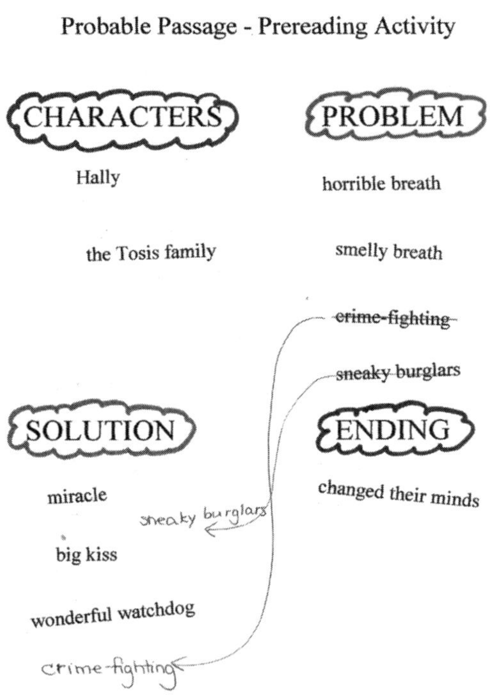

FIGURE 1.4. Probable passage: prereading activity.

Probable Passage

Hally is a character who has horrible and smelly breath. ^The Tosis family came to her house for dinner and smelled Hally's bad breath. A problem occurs when two sneaky burglars get in Hally's house.

After that, a miracle happens. Next, Hally got a wonderful watchdog. The problem is solved when a man falls in love with her and gives her a big kiss and her ^bad breath goes away.

The story ends when the two burglars changed their minds when they saw Hally got a wonderful watchdog.

FIGURE 1.5. Probable passage prediction.

- Be immersed in vocabulary study.
- Learn words through multiple exposures in multiple texts.

The vocabulary self-selection strategy (Haggard, 1986) approach builds on these principles. When using this strategy, students choose the words they want to learn, share their rationale for selecting words, and then agree upon words for a classroom collection. The steps follow:

1. *Selecting the words.* Students go through their assigned reading and identify one word they want to learn more about.
2. *Defining the words.* Students are asked to nominate one word for a classroom list. The words are recorded on a projector or board while the teacher leads a discussion of the meaning. Dictionaries may be checked to verify meanings.
3. *Finalizing the word list.* The word list is narrowed by eliminating words that are similar or that are already known. The final list of words is redefined and their meanings are added to the students' vocabulary journal.
4. *Extending word knowledge.* Follow-up activities are provided to extend word knowledge. Children are given ample opportunities to use words in their reading and writing.

The National Reading Panel (2000) concluded that a combination of methods, rather than one single method, leads to the best learning.

RESOURCES

There are a variety of good resources that a principal can provide to teachers. *Teaching Vocabulary in All Classrooms* (Blachowicz & Fisher, 2006) is filled with many practical activities, as is *Vocabulary Instruction: Research to Practice* (Baumann & Kame'enui, 2004).

Comprehension Instruction Begins in the Early Grades

How well do students understand what they are reading? And how do teachers "teach" comprehension? Even if all children received effective early reading instruction, there would still be a need for strong reading instruction emphasizing comprehension. A recent Rand report (Snow, 2002) found that "some . . . 3rd grade readers will progress on their own to proficiency in reading, but many will not. Many will need explicit, well-designed instruction in reading comprehension to continue making progress" (p. 2). Unfortunately, in too many classrooms, comprehension is taught by asking a variety of questions during and after reading. Some would argue that this questioning is important to ensure that students understand what they read. Most reading researchers would see a different model, one that is used in many classrooms today. Good readers are actively engaged when they read, so that they monitor their own comprehension. That engagement is evident from their first good experience with a story, whether it is a story they are reading or a story that is being read to them. In fact, the National Reading Panel (2000) states that there is data to suggest that comprehension is enhanced when readers are actively engaged. What are the best ways to develop this engagement so that students get the big ideas from their texts?

Again, the work of the National Reading Panel is helpful. The panel found that (1) comprehension instruction should be explicit; (2) comprehension can be improved by teaching children to use specific comprehension strategies; and (3) teachers should teach students to use a combination of strategies rather than just one strategy. The panel identified seven key instructional strategies for readers that appear to have a solid scientific basis.

1. Comprehension monitoring, during which children learn to be aware of their own understanding as they read
2. Cooperative learning, where students learn strategies together
3. The use of graphic and semantic organizers (including story maps)
4. Question answering
5. Question generating

6. Story structure analysis
7. Summarization

The panel also found that when students are able to use these strategies appropriately, they are more adept at recall, answering questions, generating questions, and summarizing texts.

The Rand Report (Snow, 2002) on comprehension supports these findings. Among its findings are the following:

- Metacognitive strategies can improve reading comprehension. Good readers understand that they must read for a purpose and monitor their understanding as they read. Explicit instruction in such strategies as questioning, summarizing, and using graphic organizers especially helps struggling readers.
- Students are more motivated when they are given challenging tasks, choices, and the opportunity to work in collaborative groups.

There are a variety of strategies that can be used to support the recommendations of the National Reading Panel and Rand Report in this regard. One of the more widely researched is reciprocal teaching, developed by Palinscar and Brown (1986).

Reciprocal Teaching

Reciprocal teaching is a discussion technique based on four strategies: predicting, questioning, clarifying, and summarizing (see Table 1.4). These four strategies are taught by modeling, guiding, and applying the strategies while reading. The strategies can be used in whole-group discussions, during guided-reading groups, in tutoring sessions with individuals, and in literature circles. Eventually, students learn to use the strategies by themselves and can takes on the roles of predictor, questioner, clarifier, and summarizer during group discussion. Even peer tutors can use these strategies as they work with younger students.

Transactional Strategies

Transactional strategy instruction (TSI) builds on the work of Palinscar and Brown (1986). Pressley and his colleagues (Pressley, 2006) developed this model to take into account the rich interaction that is needed among students and between teachers and students in order for comprehension to be effective. It is a flexible framework for teaching comprehension that can be used in whole-class, small-group, or one-on-one instruction. There are four components to TSI: explicit teaching of comprehension strategies instruction, the gradual release of responsibility to the students, collaborative learning, and discussions.

TABLE 1.4. Reciprocal Teaching Strategies

Strategy	Definition	Language used	Rationale
Predicting	Previewing the text in order to determine what happens next	*I think . . .* *I wonder if . . .* *I suppose . . .* *I predict . . .*	Helps students set a purpose for reading.
Questioning	Generating questions for someone else as they read (teacher or student)	*Who . . .* *What . . .* *When . . .* *Where . . .* *Why . . .*	Helps students focus on the text as they read, in order to generate a question.
Clarifying	Identifying difficult parts of the text (including words)	*I didn't understand . . .* *I can't figure this out . . .* *That part doesn't make sense . . .*	Helps students monitor their own understanding of the text as they identify difficult parts or words.
Summarizing	Recalling and arranging in order the important parts of the text	*The most important part in this story was . . .* *The main characters are . . .* *The problem in the story is . . .*	Helps improve overall comprehension of text.

While using some of the strategies of reciprocal teaching, TSI begins with teacher explanations and modeling of strategies. TSI emphasizes the following strategies:

- Predicting
- Questioning
- Constructing mental images
- Seeking clarifications
- Responding to the text based on prior knowledge
- Summarizing
- Interpreting

Pressley (2006) and Brown (2008) present compelling evidence of the positive effect on comprehension with this approach.

Other Strategies

There are many other strategies that help students comprehend text, even if not used in a framework such as reciprocal teaching or transactional strategies instruction.

The use of story grammars, directed–reading–thinking activities (DRTAs), know–want to know–learn (KWL), think-alouds, and graphic organizers are powerful strategies than can help students learn how to "think" while they read. Pressley's research (2006) suggests that when strategies such as these are taught, modeled, reinforced, and practiced, students' comprehension increases.

Principals should look for instruction in classrooms that emphasizes strategies for three phases, *before reading, during reading,* and *after reading.* The stage setting that occurs *before reading* is important to activate students' prior knowledge about the text they are about to read. Whether dealing with fiction or nonfiction, there are strategies that are helpful before students read a text. Many of them can be found in the resources list that follows.

The second phase emphasizes the importance of supporting students' focus *during reading,* and the third phase stresses the need for follow-up *after reading.* Many excellent teachers use strategies that connect the *after reading* phase with the *before reading* phase. The anticipation guide shown in Figure 1.6 is an example of this. The student filled this guide out before reading, then returned after reading to fill it out and note the page with the evidence supporting her answer.

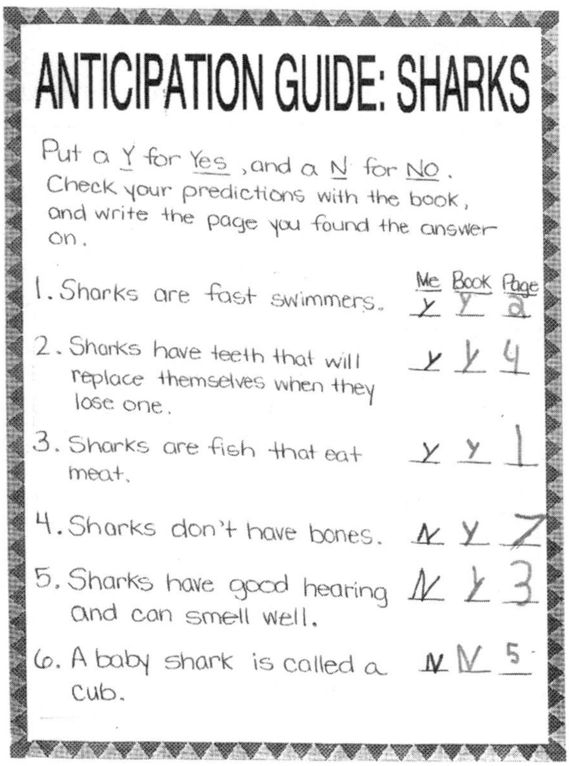
ANTICIPATION GUIDE: SHARKS

Put a Y for Yes, and a N for NO.
Check your predictions with the book, and write the page you found the answer on.

	Me	Book	Page
1. Sharks are fast swimmers.	Y	Y	2
2. Sharks have teeth that will replace themselves when they lose one.	Y	Y	4
3. Sharks are fish that eat meat.	Y	Y	1
4. Sharks don't have bones.	N	Y	7
5. Sharks have good hearing and can smell well.	N	Y	3
6. A baby shark is called a cub.	N	N	5

FIGURE 1.6. Anticipation guide.

RESOURCES

There are several books available that are good resources for teaching comprehension. Principals should consider *Reading Comprehension: Strategies for Independent Learners* (Blachowicz & Ogle, 2008) as an important resource. For principals who want their teachers to learn more about reciprocal teaching, *Reciprocal teaching at work: Strategies for improving reading comprehension* (Oczkus, 2003) is filled with concrete activities to help teachers get started. At the very least, principals should ensure that there are ample professional development opportunities for their staff.

GOOD LITERACY INSTRUCTION OCCURS ACROSS ALL CURRICULAR AREAS

Stories (fiction) account for a disproportionate amount of reading material in elementary schools. Yet, the opposite is true at the secondary level, where much of the reading is nonfiction (or informational) text. By the twelfth grade, much of what a student reads will be nonfiction (or informational) text. This shift in reading has actually been recognized by the National Assessment of Educational Progress (NAEP), which will assess students in both types of reading—fiction and nonfiction—starting in 2009. This new assessment will occur for students as early as fourth grade and will have an equal amount of literary and informational reading assessment. How do schools prepare elementary students for a different type of reading?

There has been ample evidence that teachers should teach reading and writing in all subjects areas and in all classrooms. Students should have ample opportunity to practice comprehension strategies in their science and social studies classes, not just in English language arts. A report from the National Association of School Boards of Education (Haynes, 2007) argues for such instruction, stating that literacy instruction should be "infused" throughout the curriculum and that schools should provide training and support to help teachers.

Moore, Moore, Cunningham, and Cunningham (2003) provide a strong rationale for integrating literacy learning with other curriculum areas:

1. Learning in any subject area requires the use of language, primarily reading and writing.
2. Schools and society are demanding increased levels of literacy learning, and learning across the curriculum provides more instruction in literacy at a critical time.
3. Children will be more motivated to learn when they are presented with material in an actual subject matter that is meaningful to them.
4. Connecting literacy with other content areas reinforces learning in all areas.

Reading and writing should be taught throughout the day. This not only increases comprehension in the various disciplines, but it also helps children make connections between their subject areas. As one teacher states, "I aim to get my students to . . . not keep the things they learn separate from one another, but to intertwine the different bits of knowledge."

The relationship is cyclical: Incorporating reading and writing into content classes improves comprehension, but incorporating content into reading and writing classes also improves reading and writing. If a student has already studied the Inuit cultures in social studies class, for example, it will much easier to understand a story book that has Inuit cultures in it.

In the Rand research report (Snow, 2002), one of the key findings is that comprehension is enhanced when teachers connect comprehension strategy instruction with in-depth learning of content in various disciplines. Once students learn that these strategies are tools for understanding their text, they become more purposeful in how they use them.

Learn the Differences between Fiction and Nonfiction Reading

None of this research should surprise us as educators. After all, the type of reading that occurs in a science classroom is very different from reading that may be encountered in a basal reading program. Nonfiction (or informational) textbooks provide unique challenges to readers, including the following:

- The sequence of events are often not in order.
- There may be abrupt shifts in the topic.
- There may be an abundance of material covered in a chapter, resulting in information overload.
- The information may include far too many details, with little depth on a topic.
- The vocabulary and/or pictures may not be explained well.
- Pictures and maps on the page may not be related to the text.

The differences between fiction and nonfiction text are summarized in Table 1.5.

What do these differences mean for the principal? First and foremost, the principal needs to provide leadership to ensure that all teachers are trained in reading strategies that are appropriate for their discipline. The most obvious way to do this is through professional development that is continuous throughout the year (see Chapter 3). This is an area, however, in which principals can model strategies to teachers, so that they can "walk the talk" with their teachers. Paired reading, discussed later in this chapter, is an excellent strategy for the principal to model with his or her teachers.

TABLE 1.5. The Difference between Fiction and Nonfiction Texts

Fiction	Nonfiction
Tells a story.	Provides information.
Vocabulary is general and more "everyday."	Vocabulary is specialized by discipline.
Reader identifies with characters.	Reader interacts with subject matter.
Plot holds reader's attention.	Organization of the text holds reader's attention.
Stories relate to reader's experiences.	Text often has unfamiliar abstract concepts.
Writing style is elaborate.	Writing style is very concise and heavy with content.
Entertains the reader and is written in more personal style.	Expands reader's knowledge and is written in impersonal style.
Allows rapid reading, with scanning and omission of some parts.	Requires slower reading, with a constant need to adjust rate.
Words convey most of the meaning.	Graphic aids, such as charts, tables, and maps, convey meaning.

Form a School Literacy Team

A school literacy team should be composed of the school's reading personnel, including reading specialists, media specialists, and Title I teachers and representatives from other curricular areas, such as social studies, science, and math. After researching the variety of strategies that can be used in subject-area classrooms, the team should develop a plan for infusing reading strategies throughout the school. This team should address such topics as the differences between fiction and nonfiction reading as well as the variety of strategies that can be used in content classrooms. This team should also evaluate the effectiveness of any planned training. School literacy teams are discussed further in Chapter 2.

RESOURCES

There are many websites that have an abundance of material in the area of content reading. Louisiana Public Broadcasting has developed a professional developmental series on literacy that includes handouts, lessons, resources, and clips (available at *www.litandlearn.org*). The University of Virginia Reading Quest site has a variety of strategies and handouts available for use in social studies classrooms (see *www.readingquest.org*). A book mentioned earlier, *Reading Comprehension: Strategies for Independent Learners* (Blachowicz & Ogle, 2008), is also an excellent resource for professional development.

READING AND WRITING FOR MEANING CANNOT BE OVEREMPHASIZED

While the oral and written language systems are different, there are some important parallels. When children learn to talk, for example, they have a powerful motivator for doing so: There are people around them who are talking, and they want to learn to communicate too. And what are the first words that children say? Often they are words that have a lot of meaning to them: words like *mama, dada,* and *bottle* are among their first. Why? Children naturally want to communicate something of meaning to people in their environment.

It is no different with the written language system. Children should be exposed to meaningful text from the moment they start to read and even before. Having students reading or writing stories that make little sense is not valuable for them. How does a teacher ensure that meaning is emphasized?

There are numerous examples of how teachers create these meaningful reading and writing experiences for their students. Often, teachers create group stories with their classrooms. Each story that is composed becomes part of a collection of stories available for students to read.

Teachers also provide these meaningful experiences with field trips, special visitors, or special experiences at the school. A first-grade teacher, for example, brought a large teddy bear into her classroom and led the children in a discussion and a follow-up writing exercise about the bear (Figure 1.7).

A second-grade teacher led a discussion about principals' week and had her children compose essays on the role of a principal (Figure 1.8).

Fluffy Brad Bear

Fluffy Brad is cute.
Fluffy is nice.
She felt soft.
Fluffy felt hard on her head.
She is pretty because her eyes shine.
Fluffy is brown.
She has one black eye.
She feels mushy and big.
Fluffy will eat eggs.

FIGURE 1.7. First-grade student writing sample.

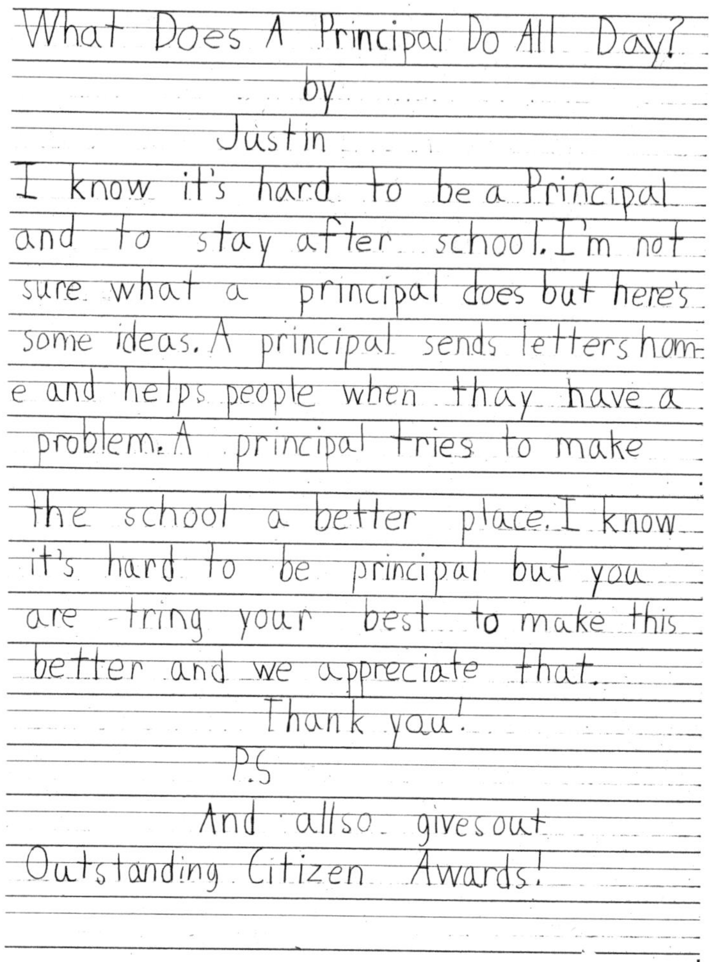

What Does A Principal Do All Day?
by
Justin
I know it's hard to be a Principal and to stay after school. I'm not sure what a principal does but here's some ideas. A principal sends letters hom-e and helps people when thay have a problem. A principal tries to make the school a better place. I know it's hard to be principal but you are tring your best to make this better and we appreciate that.
Thank you!
P.S
And allso gives out Outstanding Citizen Awards!

(continued)

FIGURE 1.8. "What Principals Do" letters.

While teaching the form of letters, a third-grade teacher had her students practice writing letters to people in their school. After sufficient practice, they sent letters to their principal. An example of one of these letters is seen in Figure 1.9.

Why are these practices important? Children are learning that reading and writing are important ways to communicate with others. This emphasis on communication is an important aspect of the "meaning" principles.

There are other ways to emphasize meaning for children. Events that promote schoolwide literacy activities give every child an opportunity to participate in a meaningful event that will be long remembered. Character dress-up days, reading of student-authored pieces on the school television, student book reviews

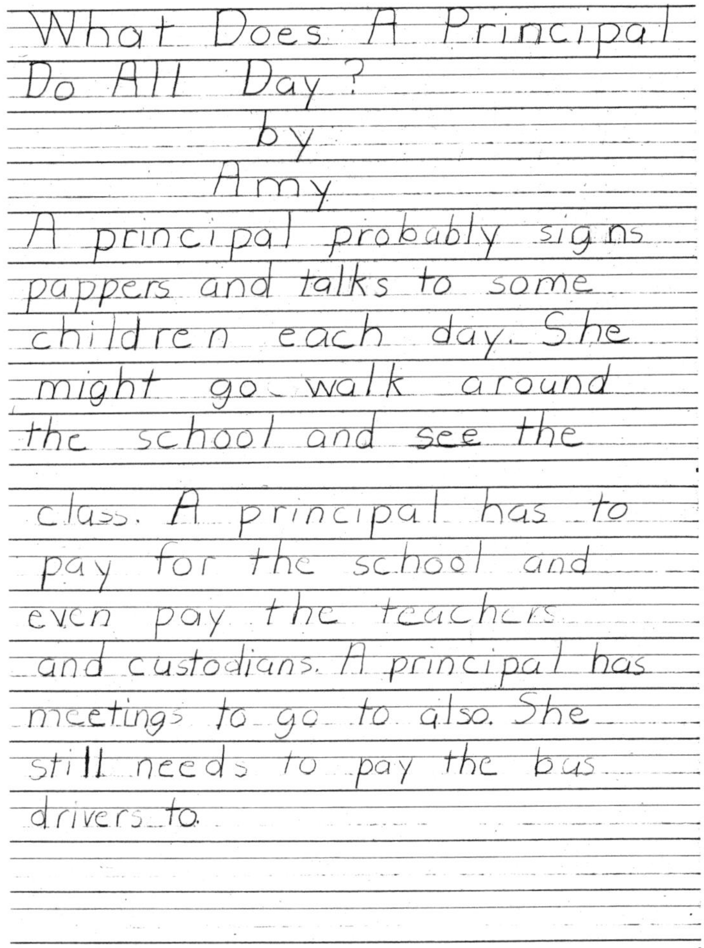

What Does A Principal Do All Day?
by
Amy
A principal probably signs pappers and talks to some children each day. She might go walk around the school and see the class. A principal has to pay for the school and even pay the teachers and custodians. A principal has meetings to go to also. She still needs to pay the bus drivers to.

FIGURE 1.8. *(cont.)*

published in school newsletters or placed inside library books, and "I read to the principal" programs all stress the importance of making meaningful literacy connections for students.

DISCUSSION AND OTHER ORAL LANGUAGE STRATEGIES ARE CRITICAL

A strong literacy classroom will have a lot of talk and discussion about books and other literacy events throughout the day. This talk and discussion is important in classrooms. This country is increasingly more polarized and divided over issues

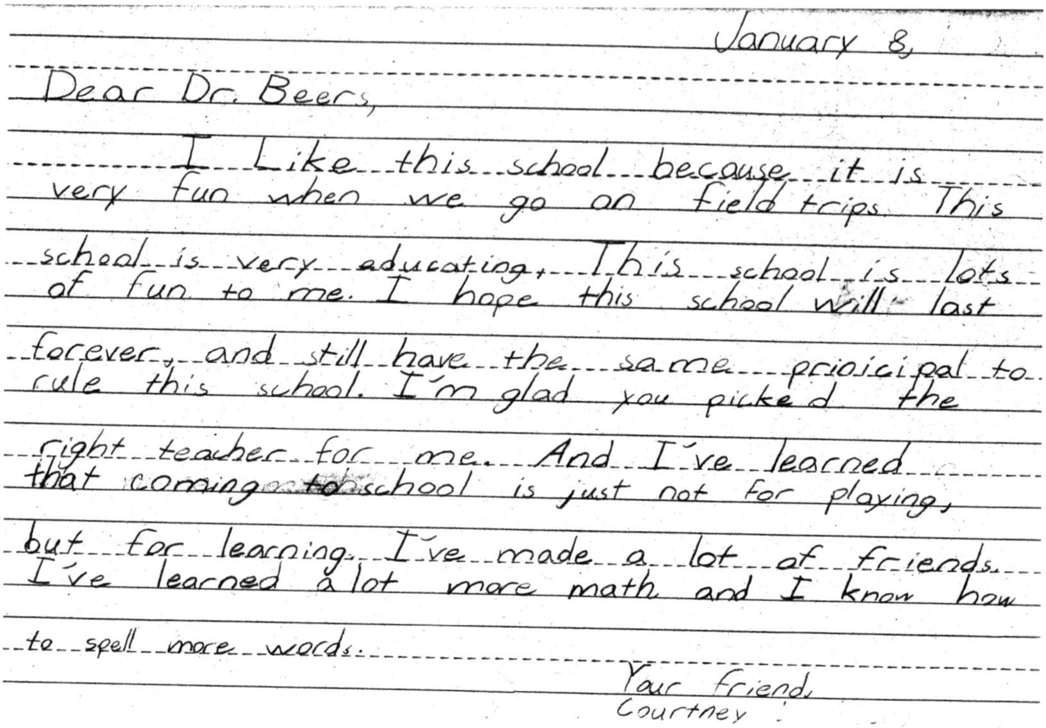

January 8,

Dear Dr. Beers,

I Like this school because it is very fun when we go on field trips. This school is very educating. This school is lots of fun to me. I hope this school will last forever, and still have the same prioicipal to rule this school. I'm glad you picked the right teacher for me. And I've learned that coming to school is just not for playing, but for learning. I've made a lot of friends. I've learned a lot more math and I know how to spell more words.

Your Friend,
Courtney

FIGURE 1.9. Letter to the principal.

that matter. Adults often do not engage in civil conversations where it is safe to disagree with the opinions of others. Instead, there are often talking heads on the television yelling at each other with increasingly loud voices to get their opinions across to their "challenger." This is not conversation, nor is this a helpful role model for students. Students need to learn how to express their opinions, listen to each other, and disagree with each other.

Communicating well with a variety of people is an increasingly important skill. Students today will live and work in a society that will require the ability to communicate well with a variety of people. The minority portion of the workforce is expected to double by 2020, while the majority portion will decline by 25% (The National Center for Public Policy and Higher Education, November, 2005).

Oral language has other more immediate purposes. Much language grows between the ages of 5 and 10. Knowing this, teachers must plan opportunities for children to talk in their classrooms. This is especially critical for children who are not comfortable with "school language" and have come from homes where either English is spoken as a second language or where there is a cultural variation that is not viewed as acceptable by school norms.

Talk and listening in classrooms also promote better comprehension as well as more critical thinking and problem solving. Palinscar and Brown's work (1986) on reciprocal teaching showed that students had better reading comprehension when they engaged in structured conversations about text. Almasi (1995) found higher-level thinking when teachers used discussion in classrooms.

Oral Language Strategies

There are a variety of ways that principals can help teachers encourage more talk in their classrooms. As teachers become more comfortable with talk in their classrooms, they will find many ways to enhance the quantity and quality of talk.

➢ Encourage kindergarten and first-grade children to have "*show and tell*," but in small groups rather than one large group. Reducing the size of the group allows more children to present and encourages more children to listen to the speaker. Consider volunteering in your teachers' classrooms at this time. Parent volunteers and assistants could also help.

➢ Encourage all teachers to provide shared-risk activities. Not all children feel comfortable expressing their own points of view. By providing shared-risk activities, children report out to the class as part of a group. Examples of shared-risk activities include think–pair–share and opinion trios.

➢ Demonstrate to teachers the advantage of using a strategy such as *paired reading* (Dansereau 1986). This strategy is advantageous because all students are asked to talk about a text with a partner. During a paired reading exercise, students work in pairs with two distinct roles: that of a reporter who summarizes and that of a responder who questions. The reading assignment (which is read by the class ahead of time) is divided into four sections. Each of the four sections is then subdivided in half. Directions for paired reading are seen in Figure 1.10. This particular strategy is one that is easy for a principal to learn and demonstrate.

➢ Providing opportunities for teachers to learn more about cooperative learning is also a useful strategy for promoting meaningful talk in classrooms. The use of *expert groups,* in particular, is a strategy that engages all students. This strategy, developed by Aronson and his students (1978), reassigns students from their home group to an expert group. Each expert group is assigned one or two aspects of a topic (or questions) to discuss. Their goal is to reach a common understanding of these topics. After they reach an understanding, they return to their home group and present the information to the members of their home group.

➢ Demonstrate the use of *discussion webs* (Alverman, 1991) as a tool to promote discussion. After reading a selection, the teacher writes a thought-provoking question that can be answered with a "yes" or "no." Students are paired off to discuss the question and are asked to list four or five reasons why the question could

Paired Reading Strategy

The paired reading strategy involves all students talking about the text. In paired reading:

- Students first read the entire chapter or article.
- The teacher divides the text into four sections.
- Each section is then divided into two sections, called A and B.
- Students are paired for a second reading.
- Each member of the pair has a distinct role for each section: that of reporter and that of responder.
  - The reporter reads the section and summarizes the section for his or her partner, in his or her own words.
  - The responder reads the section and asks the reporter questions that clarify. (e.g. "What does that mean?" "What about. . .?")
- The partners choose whether they are the A or the B person.
- The A person is the reporter for the A section. The B person is the responder.
- The B person is the reporter for the B section. The A person is the responder.
- Once they are done, the pairs develop a graphic organizer and use this organizer to report out to the group.
- There will be multiple pairs reporting out on the same section. This is a way of reinforcing the material with students.

FIGURE 1.10. Directions for paired reading.

be answered either way. The pairs may then combine with another pair to discuss their reasons, modifying their lists for both responses. This group of four then considers all their reasons and tries to reach consensus on their answer to the central question. Groups may report to the whole class or write their own response. See Figure 1.11 for detailed directions for a discussion web.

The Role of Classroom Discussion

Discussion occurs in a classroom when there is an authentic conversation during which students exchange ideas, thoughts, and feelings. A discussion does not take

This involves the use of a graphic organizer with a think–pair–share.

- Teacher writes a thought-provoking yes/no question in the middle of the web.
- Students work in pairs to discuss and list reasons for both the yes and no response to the question underneath each response.
- Partners pair with another partner pair to compare and contrast their responses. Each partner pair then modifies and adds to their original responses.
- Students then reach consensus on their response to the question, checking those reasons that best support their response.
- The group reports out to the whole class.
- Individual students then write their own response.

Sample Questions:

Yes	Should we drill for oil off the coast of Alaska?	No
Yes	Was the Civil War a necessary war?	No
Yes	Should Jack have climbed the beanstalk a second time?	No

FIGURE 1.11. Discussion web.

place when the teachers ask a lot of questions and students take turns answering them. During a real discussion, students may offer more than one point of view and are willing to respond to different points of view. Discussions may be teacher-led or student-led. Principals hold a key leadership role in encouraging teachers to promote real discussion in their classrooms.

There are several reasons why discussion is thought to be important in schools. First of all, when students engage in a discussion about a book, they have a deeper understanding of it. The benefits of discussion have been found as early as kindergarten. Morrow and Smith (1990) found that kindergarten children who engaged in small-group discussion of stories read aloud had superior story recall. Goodlad's classic study (1984) estimated that there was a 4–8% probability of finding discussion at all levels in all subject areas. Real discussion is not that easy to find in schools, yet its role is critical in establishing a literacy culture.

The following list may provide some simple but effective ways to help teachers increase discussion in their classrooms.

➤ Monitor the use of parroting in the classroom, during which teachers repeat exactly what a student says. Such a strategy, while well-intended, effectively cuts off discussion, as all eyes (and ears) focus on the teacher. After all, if the teacher is always repeating what another child says, why do other students have to listen to that child?

➤ Look at the seating arrangement to make sure the classroom is conducive to small-group discussions. If all desks and chairs are lined up in a row, there is a pretty good chance that there won't be a lot of meaningful discussion in the classroom. Instead, encourage teachers to form small groups of four to six with their children's desks.

➤ Encourage teachers to develop rules for discussion with their children. These rules could be posted in the class so that they are easily accessed when needed.

RESOURCES

A good source for teachers wanting to learn more about promoting discussion is *Lively Discussions! Fostering Engaged Reading* (Gambrell & Almasi, 1996). Staff development programs such as that offered by Junior Great Books (*www.greatbooks.org*) and the Padeia Seminar training (*www.paideia.org*) should also be considered.

DIVERSITY SHOULD BE CELEBRATED IN CLASSROOMS AND ACROSS THE SCHOOL

Schools and classrooms today reflect the great diversity in this country. That diversity continues to increase, with expectations that there will be no majority culture by the year 2050. There are projections that suggest that the minority population will increase to 63 million by the year 2030, with over 30 million African Americans and 20 million Hispanics, primarily from Central and South America. This diversity, which also includes a growing number of other cultures in schools presents a challenge to educators.

It is important for educators not just to accept diversity as a condition, but to celebrate and embrace the various cultures within schools. One school where one of us worked had 37 different languages reflected in the student population.

Culture is reflected in a variety of ways: self-identity, the communication system, dress and appearance, food, awareness of time, relationships, values, and beliefs and attitudes. A school that is aware of the various ways that culture is expressed will begin to see the need for a multicultural approach. In particular, once school staff members learn that students and their communities have different values and beliefs, they also can begin to accommodate these values and beliefs in everything they do. Staff members who work in such an environment will see the positive traits that each culture brings to the school rather than focus on the negative challenges.

How do schools begin to embrace this diversity? Banks (1999) lists several benchmarks for schools to use as they try to develop effective environments for multiculturalism. These benchmarks include the following:

- A policy statement that supports diversity
- Staff with positive attitudes and expectations toward all students
- Staff that reflect the ethnic and cultural diversity of their students
- A curriculum that is inclusive of different perspectives and points of view
- Parent involvement that reflects the changing characteristics of families and parents within the community
- Teaching strategies that allow students to express themselves and work cooperatively within the classroom
- Teaching materials that reflect a range of ethnic and cultural groups and embed these perspectives throughout the materials
- Continuous monitoring of multicultural experiences through classroom visits as well as analysis of test and performance data

The literacy classroom is an important place to begin with as many multicultural experiences as possible. Textbooks and trade books in classrooms should reflect the wide variety of cultures within the school and community. Part of the rationale for this is common sense: Children can identify with stories that reflect their own situations. Beyond this, however, providing this type of literature creates a transition between home and school. In addition, providing a variety of multicultural experiences allows children to see powerful role models and models of writers who value their cultures.

The principal should pay attention to how children learn about the different cultures. While the celebration of certain holidays may be useful, these celebrations should never substitute for the learning of different cultures within the context of academics. While studying World War II, for example, children could learn about a variety of different groups in this country who were affected by the war: women, African Americans, German Americans, and Asian Americans. While studying the Civil War, the contributions of African Americans could be highlighted. There are a variety of supplemental resources that can be used in this regard.

CONCLUSIONS

This chapter has focused on several key principles of good literacy instruction: (1) the need to understand the developmental stages of literacy; (2) the importance of balanced literacy instruction that addresses phonemic awareness, vocabulary study, word study, fluency, and comprehension; (3) the importance of offering literacy experiences in all curricular areas; (4) the need for meaningful literacy activities; (5) the role of discussion and oral language in the literacy classroom; and (6) the need to celebrate the diversity of students and staff within the school. While each area has been presented with discussion, it would be difficult to present these topics in any depth within the context of just one chapter. It is our hope that the principal, as the instructional leader, will consult the abundance of resources to learn about any of these areas in more depth.

LOOKING AHEAD

It is important to recognize and support the complexity of a strong literacy program. Strong literacy programs do not grow without strong leadership from the principal. As principals strive to establish the components of a strong literacy program in schools, they will need to attend to the culture and climate. A strong literacy culture will ensure that everything the school believes in is supported and enhanced throughout the day. Our next chapter will focus on ways to establish this literacy culture.

CHAPTER 2

ESTABLISHING A LITERACY CULTURE IN SCHOOL

Culture and leadership are two sides of the same coin.
—SCHEIN (2004, p. 23)

The bottom line for leaders is that if they do not become conscious of the cultures in which they are embedded, those cultures will manage them.
—SCHEIN (2004, p. 23)

What do visitors sense when they come into schools? Believe it or not, they sense something, but may not be able to articulate it. They may sense that this is a fun and lively place to be. They may sense that this is a serious workplace. They may even sense that this is a challenging school with a lot of problem areas. As principals, we don't like to think that such "sensing" is legitimate. Those who have studied school climate and culture, however, would tell us a different story. In fact, if these visitors, whether community members or school employees, were to share their observations and feelings, a picture of the school would begin to emerge. These feelings that visitors have reflect a piece of the school's culture. Every school has its own unique characteristics, and visitors can sense these by listening and observing.

School culture generally refers to the *long-term* and deeply embedded patterns of norms, values, beliefs, and assumptions (Deal and Peterson, 2002, 2003) that not only guide behaviors but also give a school its identity. Schein (2004) suggests that the term *culture* should be used for the deeper assumptions and beliefs that operate unconsciously and shape how individuals in that culture will respond. Visitors to a school often infer things about the culture by the way the school is decorated and maintained, by the manner in which everyone interacts (parents, students, teachers, staff, and administration), and by beliefs that are expressed by the staff.

Those like Schein (2004) who have studied school culture have found there are some common elements to a culture. There are strongly held beliefs and values. There are stories that are told that communicate what the organization is about. There are heroes and heroines within the organization whose accomplishments reflect those values. There are rituals and ceremonies that reinforce the values. Finally, there are key players who communicate the values to others in the organization, both through actions and through words.

The *climate* in school reflects school culture. School climate refers to the *short-term* changeable aspects of the school's physical and psychological environment. The climate of a school is evident when a visitor walks into the school. Do the students and staff greet visitors? Is the office staff inviting and friendly? Are there comfortable places to sit and wait for scheduled appointments? Are visitors welcome in classrooms? All of these aspects are a reflection of school climate. Many researchers have noted that school climate has a high correlation to student achievement.

School climate is complex, and there may not always be agreement about what contributes to school climate. Schools often identify different components that contribute to school climate . . . things they want to change. Some of these components obviously reflect the values of those in the school. Some frequently mentioned components include the appearance of the school, the relationships among staff members, the relationships between staff and students, the relationships between parents and staff, the ways in which decisions are made, the physical environment for learning, and the relationship between the school and community.

Researchers have identified a number of characteristics in effective schools that were climate- or culture-based. Some of the most frequently mentioned characteristics in these studies included the following:

- High expectations for all students, which results in an optimistic attitude for each student
- Student-centeredness that helps meet the needs of each student
- Focused mission, which provides staff with a sense of purpose
- Rewards and incentives for accomplishments of teachers and students
- A well-maintained physical environment that displays students' work
- Frequent monitoring of progress
- A high level of community support

In a study of secondary schools, Roueche and Baker (1986) found five key organizational characteristics in highly successful schools. While their study focused on secondary schools, their characteristics are pertinent to all levels of schooling. These five key organizational characteristics reflect the culture and climate of the school, with a particular emphasis on the principal's leadership.

- *Leadership by example* is prevalent, and staff members in these schools notice those actions. Principals in these schools often spend most of their time in the halls and classrooms, not in their offices.
- Principals in these schools perceive themselves to be *instructional leaders* and are committed to observing classroom instruction.
- The school is committed to effective *professional development* of its staff. Teachers in these schools are involved in planning and implementing the training that is offered.
- There is *accountability through evaluation*. Teachers welcome efforts to evaluate and improve their effectiveness.
- There is more *community involvement*, with more active parent associations and parents volunteering and visiting classrooms frequently. Similarly, staff members are encouraged to become involved in community projects.

ASPECTS OF ENVIRONMENT THAT AFFECT SCHOOL CLIMATE

The principal's role is powerful and essential in ensuring that a positive climate is built in the school. After all, climate can affect the morale, productivity, and satisfaction of staff. The components that many educators view as part of school climate can be grouped into four areas: the physical environment, the social environment, the affective environment, and the academic environment. (Best Practices Brief, 2004). Approaching school climate through these areas allows the development of a more comprehensive and cohesive approach to school environment.

The *physical environment* should be welcoming and conducive to learning. This category refers to all those items that include the physical and material aspects of school, including how well the building is maintained and cared for, whether the grounds and classrooms are clean, whether classrooms are visible and inviting, whether staff have ample textbooks and supplies, and whether students feel safe and comfortable.

The *social environment* is shaped by the types of communication and interaction at school. In a positive social environment, teachers are collegial and open in their communication process. Parents and teachers frequently work together as partners. Staff members are part of decision making and they are open to students' suggestions. They are comfortable with conflict resolution and expressing their opinions in a supportive and trusting atmosphere.

As principals look at their school, they may want to take note of the frequency and types of interactions among staff members, students, and parents. Are students and teachers engaged in informal conversations? Are parent opinions and suggestions valued and acted upon by staff members? Do staff members feel comfortable disagreeing with each other, but in a positive and constructive manner? Do staff members talk with each other throughout the day and throughout the building? All of these observations can contribute to the social environment, which affects school climate.

The *affective environment* refers to those aspects of the environment that promote a sense of belonging. When the affective environment is positive, students, staff, and parents feel respected and valued. They feel that they are important members of the school community and that their input is respected and valued. In schools where there is a positive affective environment, there is a high degree of trust and respect among staff members. The staff and students are friendly to visitors and to each other. When staff members are talking, they are talking constructively about the people and events at the school. School events are well attended by the staff. This kind of affective environment contributes to a high degree of morale within a school. For the purposes of our discussion, we have combined the social and affective aspects of environment. This combination allows us to focus on staff and students without trying to differentiate which is social versus affective.

The final aspect of school climate is referred to as the *academic environment* that promotes learning. In a school that has a positive academic environment, there are high expectations for all students and all students are expected to succeed. In this environment, teachers monitor the progress of their students regularly and make adjustments in their teaching accordingly. When assessments are conducted, the results are shared with students and their parents on a regular basis. In a school where there is a strong academic environment, the achievements of students are positively reinforced in both public and private ways.

The Physical Environment

Look around your school through the lens of a parent or community member. Often, the first place the visitor comes is to the office. For many visitors, this is the only place that they visit. What does the office look like? Is there a welcoming place that visitors report to? If they have an appointment, can they sit comfortably and read material while they wait? Is it clear where the restrooms are if visitors need to use them?

The rest of the school is important as well. Is the school kept clean? Is there litter in the restrooms, hallways, stairwells, or classrooms? Are there signs indicating where various classrooms and grade levels are housed? Are the hallways decorated with a variety of student work? Can visitors look into classrooms, or have teachers covered door windows with paper, as though they are hiding something? If there are elderly visitors (as often happens in many districts with retirement communities), is the building easy to negotiate?

The outside of the building is also important. Are the school grounds attractive and well-maintained? In some schools, children maintain school gardens that are planted by members of local garden clubs. In other schools, parent volunteers help with planting seasonal flowers and bulbs near the entrance. Each of these small steps communicates to the visitor that this is a special place for children.

These are only some of the ways that the physical environment reflects the climate in a school. As authors, we have visited hundreds of schools and found that a brief walk through the school with a principal can reveal whether the principal cares about the physical environment. Some principals walk through the school and ignore the little signs of decay: the crumbled pieces of paper in the halls, the curled-up student work that has been hung in the hall for too long, the lack of soap in the restrooms. The principal who stoops down to pick up a piece of paper in the hall or who stops a teacher in the hallway to complement the display of student work is sending a much more powerful message than any written memo can ever send.

The Social and Affective Environment

How do principals nurture a positive social and affective environment? Think about all the opportunities that principals have to set the tone for this environment. Many principals make a practice of greeting their *students* at the beginning of each day, as soon as they come off the bus or walk into the building. Finding a central place to stand and greet students is not difficult, takes no more than 10 to 15 minutes, and sends an important message: "I'm glad you're here and I care enough about you to be here to greet you." In one school we visited, the principal not only greeted students, she made it a point to make comments to several students as they came into the building, noticing a new jacket, a book in their hands, or a conversation with their teacher. These comments became this principal's special way to promote a relationship with students. Some additional ideas for promoting positive relationships with students include the following:

- Make it a practice to invite small groups of students to the office for lunch. Make the lunch casual and conversational. One principal made a point to schedule these lunches so that every child in the school had the opportunity to have lunch with the principal.
- Consider rewarding students who have had good days with a book reading at the end of the day. Each teacher could send one student during the last thirty minutes of school once a week.

Another principal made it a daily practice to be in the office when *parents* picked up their children. This was an important time for the parents to see the principal and to have informal conversations about the day or the events in school. During this time, parents also got to see the principal more informally. This informal meeting allowed an exchange of ideas that built relationships over the course of the year. Other ideas for building relationships with parents include the following:

➤ Consider calling parents when their child has done something positive: perhaps he shared something with a classmate, perhaps she helped someone on a project; perhaps he improved in a subject. Calling parents for positive things lets them know the principal cares about their children. Often the only time they hear from us is when their child has done something "wrong."

➤ Ask faculty members to call parents after the first week of school, just to share something positive about each child.

➤ Consider sending occasional postcards to parents to notify them of something positive that has happened. One principal sent postcards out once a month to the parents of two children in each classroom. The postcard may have noted that the child read a book exceptionally well, had done well on a test, or had behaved well in the cafeteria. Over the course of the year, each child's parents received one such postcard from the principal.

Promoting relationships among *staff* is of equal importance to ensuring a positive environment. While many might talk about social events to promote these relationships, the quality of daily interactions among staff is much more important than monthly social events. How can this relationship be promoted?

Many schools have committees that help promote a sense of collegiality within the school. The types of committees can vary, depending on the needs of the school. There can be committees for home–school relations, school discipline, school climate, and school improvement, to name a few. These committees should include all staff members, not just faculty. Perhaps the teacher's assistant who has strong community connections might know just the right way to get parents more involved.

It is important that committees are given the authority to make decisions along with a budget to implement some decisions. In one school, for example, the home–school relations committee decided that they wanted to send postcards to the parents of every student who showed improvement in reading on their report cards. That committee had a small budget and spent it on postcards, as they believed this small act would have a big effect on the students in the school. They were right.

In addition to empowering staff through committees, it is important for the principal to let the staff know that they are valued. This can be done through a public "thank-you" at faculty meetings or in school newsletters as well through private notes placed in staff mailboxes. Sometimes the expressions can be done in a 1-minute exchange in the hallway. These expressions of appreciation are an important way to let staff know that the many things they do to make a difference in the school.

Finally, the daily interactions with staff throughout the school are important. Once principals know the staff, they learn enough about them to have brief but meaningful conversations. Every staff member has a story to tell, as they all have their own lives and all the challenges that come with these lives. Principals who know enough about their staff can ask one staff member how her son is doing while another staff member might be asked about his new house. Brief conversations—but meaningful.

All of these suggestions assume that the principal is actively moving about the school and frequently interacting with students and staff. Other ways that principals promote a strong affective environment, one in which all members of the school community feel valued, include the following:

- Visiting every classroom every day, even if it is just for a few minutes
- Creating a suggestion box for students, staff, and parents
- Promoting more student cooperation through the use of cooperative learning strategies
- Promoting more teacher collegiality through team teaching, common planning times, and teacher exchanges
- Developing staff–student mentorship programs, in which each at-risk child has a staff member who mentors him or her
- Placing "cookie coupons" that can be redeemed in the school cafeteria in teachers' mailboxes to recognize those who have done something above and beyond
- Providing staff development on issues related to cultural and ethnic diversity to promote an understanding of all cultures
- Arranging for substitutes and other resource teachers to cover classes in various teams to provide extended planning time
- Teaching a class or reading a book to a class for a teacher who needs extra time to work on a special project or to observe another teacher
- Holding lottery drawings at staff meetings, during which staff members have the opportunity to win a 1-hour break

The Academic Environment

How can a principal provide a strong academic environment? Among other actions we've described, the principal "walks the talk." The principal who inquires about student learning when interacting with students is walking the talk of academic environments. The principal who inquires about a class that a teacher is taking is walking the talk of academic environments. What are some additional ways principals encourage a strong academic environment? The following list is a compilation of some of the observations we made in schools where there are strong academic environments:

- They attend the staff development that the district offers its staff, as well attending as in-school staff development.
- They participate in readers' groups that are offered to staff at the school and in the district.
- They listen and talk to students about their work during their visits in classrooms.
- They listen and talk to teachers regarding their concerns about their students' achievement.
- They read special books to students rather than reward them with tangible treats.
- During their evaluation conferences with teachers, they ask questions in order to deepen their understanding of the lesson.
- They teach demonstration lessons for teachers, especially in their area of interest.
- Their newsletters and correspondence with teachers contain suggestions for a new teaching strategy or motivation technique.
- They meet frequently with the curriculum leaders in their school in order to learn as much as possible about the instructional needs in the building.
- They decentralize their budget to ensure that funds for instructional supplies are available.

There are several school climate surveys that are helpful for principals to use as they attempt to gauge the school climate in their buildings. One has been developed by the Alliance for the Study of School Climate at California State University in Los Angeles. Sample items are included in Figure 2.1. For the alliance's complete survey, visit *www.calstatela.edu/centers/schoolclimate/assessment*.

PROMOTING A STRONG LITERACY CULTURE AND CLIMATE

The principal has an exciting and demanding job. The principal is the one who teachers depend on to handle all the issues that occur during the day. Many times they want assistance with a smorgasbord of issues: discipline, instructional resources, parents, custodial needs, field trip requests, or equipment needs. Most often teachers do not ask to change the climate of the school, as they often view the climate as something that is intangible and intransient.

Yet the climate is changeable, and the principal has a critical leadership role in this area. In fact, the principal's leadership will play a pivotal role in the school's ability to establish a thriving literacy program. As a leader, the principal must

Directions: Please circle the item below that best describes the current state at your school in general. For each of the three performance levels there are three sublevels (high, middle, and low).

Physical Appearance		
Level-3	Level-2	Level-1
High Middle Low	High Middle Low	High Middle Low
Welcoming to outsiders, the school projects an identity to visitors.	Some signage for visitors as they enter the building, but images compete for attention.	Little concern for the image of the school.
Current student work is displayed to show pride and ownership by students.	Few and/or only top performances are displayed	Decades-old trophies and athletic records in dusty cases.
Faculty Relations		
Level-3	Level-2	Level-1
High Middle Low	High Middle Low	High Middle Low
Faculty commonly collaborate on matters of teaching.	Faculty are congenial to one another, and occasionally collaborate.	Faculty see other faculty as the competition.
Leadership roles are most likely performed by faculty with other faculty expressing their appreciation.	Leadership roles are accepted grudgingly by faculty, and other faculty are often suspicious of motives.	Leadership is avoided, and those who do take leadership roles are seen as traitors.
Leadership/Decisions		
Level-3	Level-2	Level-1
High Middle Low	High Middle Low	High Middle Low
Vast majority of staff members feel valued and listened to.	Selected staff members feel occasionally recognized.	Administration is seen as playing favorites.
Most of the staff has a high level of trust and respect in leadership.	Some staff have respect for leadership.	Most staff feel at odds with the leadership.
Leadership is in tune with students and community.	Leadership has selected sources of info about the community and students.	Leadership is isolated from constituents.

(continued)

FIGURE 2.1. Sample items from the Alliance for the Study of School Climate survey. From the Alliance for the Study of School Climate (2004). Copyright 2004 by the Trustees of the California State University. Reprinted by permission.

Learning/Assessment		
Level-3	Level-2	Level-1
High Middle Low	High Middle Low	High Middle Low
Instruction/assessment promotes student locus of control, sense of belonging, and sense of competence. Instruction is dynamic, involving, learner-centered, and challenging.	Instruction/assessment is most often focused on relevant learning, yet mostly rewards the high-achievers. Instruction is mostly based on relevant concepts but often appears to be busy work.	Instruction/assessment is focused on bits of knowledge that can be explained and then tested. Instruction is mostly "sit and get."
Attitude and Culture		
Level-3	Level-2	Level-1
High Middle Low	High Middle Low	High Middle Low
Students speak about the school in proud, positive terms. Most students feel listened to, represented, and like they have a voice.	Students speak of the school in neutral or mixed terms. Most students see some evidence that some students have a voice.	Students denigrate the school when they refer to it. Most students feel they have very little voice when at school.
Community Relations		
Level-3	Level-2	Level-1
High Middle Low	High Middle Low	High Middle Low
School is perceived as welcoming to all parents. Community members are regularly invited to speak in classes.	School is perceived as welcoming to certain parents. Inconvenience leads to few community members speaking in classes.	School is suspicious of why parents would want to visit. The vast majority of community members have not seen the inside of the school since they went there.

FIGURE 2.1. *(continued)*

be committed to improving the literacy climate in the building. What the principal says, and more important, what he or she does, will carry the school forward in this critical area. The principal plays a primary role by providing leadership, articulating his or her expectations, and supporting the staff and students on their literacy journey.

While general ways to improve climate have been discussed in an earlier section, this section will focus on the *literacy* culture in school. By making a conscious effort to improve the environment for literacy, principals will be enhancing the opportunities for students so that more students can be successful.

Provide Leadership

The principal is expected to walk the talk, or to lead by example. The staff looks to the principal for guidance and support. If principals demonstrate a commitment through their actions, the staff will notice. In fact, the principal's role in literacy leadership is so important that a group of leading reading experts met with the Children's Literacy Initiative (CLI) in Philadelphia in 2001 to discuss it. These experts identified nine areas of content knowledge necessary for principals providing literacy leadership:

1. *School culture:* understanding what culture is and their role in changing it
2. *Craft leaders:* knowing the leaders in literacy instruction who provide fresh ideas and useful models
3. *Children's literature:* reading quality children's literature and sharing their love of reading with staff, students, and parents
4. *Instructional models:* taking the lead to ensure that staff members understand the complexities of models of reading
5. *Curriculum:* knowing the district's literacy curriculum and making sure teachers can deliver it in a meaningful way
6. *Options for organizing time and space:* being aware of how various uses of time and space affect instruction
7. *Assessment/content standards:* using assessment data with staff and parents in a meaningful way
8. *Special interventions:* examining how support is provided to struggling readers
9. *Knowledge and research:* knowing where to find information on what works and why

As principals consider their own leadership in this area, they may want to think about the steps that they can take to demonstrate their commitment to staff members.

➢ A first step is to learn as much as possible about literacy. Principals should read some of the leading thinkers and practitioners in the field. A wealth of information can be found at the website for the International Reading Association (*www.reading.org*). Additional information can be found at the ERIC Clearinghouse (*www.reading.indiana.edu*) as well as at the website for the National Reading Panel (*www.nationalreadingpanel.org*).

➢ Consider attending professional development sessions that are geared towards the development of literacy. These sessions are often offered at district, state, and national levels. Subscribing to literacy journals such as *The Reading*

Teacher, which is filled with practical teaching strategies, is another way principals can learn more. When staff members see that their principal is interested in literacy, they will view the principal as someone who is truly committed to promoting literacy.

➢ Assess the school's current culture for literacy. What are the cultural norms at the school? Is there acceptance of the status quo? Or are staff members continually striving to improve their own understanding of literacy learning?

➢ Learn who the key players are in the school. Deal and Kennedy (2000) suggest these key players are sources of expertise that leaders should tap. Who are the longtime members of the school community? Who are the storytellers who can tell about past events? Are there gossips who keep track of all the activities and goings on? And finally, who are the underground staff who negotiate between various cliques in the school?

➢ Look for a variety of signs in the physical, social, affective, and academic environment. Is there a lot of student work displayed? Does it show evidence of students' reading and writing experiences? Do staff members participate in literacy staff development and/or readers' groups? Are there enough trade books (both fiction and nonfiction) in classrooms? Do children choose to read during their free time? Do they read at transition points during the day? The principal may want to spend time with the reading specialist or literacy coach while walking around the school and assessing various aspects of the literacy climate (see Figure 2.2).

➢ Invite staff members from other schools and districts to visit the school and provide feedback on what they notice as strengths and needs.

➢ Spend time in classrooms observing literacy strategies in all subject areas, not just in reading classes. By doing this, principals will gain insight into the professional needs that staff may have as well as knowledge about how and what students are learning in these classrooms.

➢ Consider beginning a "principal's choice" program, in which principals select one children's book a month to distribute to teachers. Inside each book is a message that explains why the book was chosen. Teachers then read the book to their classes, providing a schoolwide literacy discussion with an important message.

After they spend some time learning more about literacy and also observing the culture in the school, principals are in a better position to address ways to strengthen this culture from a knowledge and research base.

Provide a Physical Environment That Celebrates Literacy

In schools where there is a great deal of support for high levels of literacy, there is a greater chance that students will be more successful and teachers more motivated.

The Physical Environment	Strongly agree	Agree	Disagree	Strongly disagree
Children's work is displayed throughout the school, including hallways and offices.				
Student work is rotated routinely in order to ensure timely materials displays.				
Books and other reading materials are readily available in reading corners in all classrooms.				
Books and other reading materials are available for students and parents in the office and clinic.				
The principal's office exhibits students' work and children's literature.				
The principal's office is easily accessible to staff.				

The Social and Affective Environment	Strongly agree	Agree	Disagree	Strongly disagree
There are ample recognitions of students accomplishments throughout the school year.				
The principal frequently recognizes students when entering classrooms.				
The principal is actively engaged in promoting literacy.				
There are celebrations of literacy during the school year.				
There is a collaborative culture that builds on the expertise and talents of staff members.				
There is adequate time for staff to collaborate with each other on literacy issues.				
Staff members are frequently involved in decision making.				

The Academic Environment	Strongly agree	Agree	Disagree	Strongly disagree
There is a literacy leadership team that involves personnel in assessment and planning.				
Large blocks of time are provided for literacy instruction.				
Instructional time is protected from unnecessary interruptions.				
Common planning time is provided to all teams.				
Literacy is supported in all curricular areas.				
There are ample books, both fiction and nonfiction, throughout the school.				
A variety of meaningful professional opportunities about literacy are routinely provided throughout the year.				
There is enthusiasm throughout the school community for the school community of learners.				

FIGURE 2.2. Survey of literacy climate.

The physical environment, as mentioned earlier, plays a vital role in establishing a positive climate in school. Principals should talk with people in the school community and look at their school with a dispassionate eye if they really want to assess the climate. What artifacts in the physical environment would communicate a strong value for literacy?

Principals can take some simple steps to create a physical environment that shows that literacy is valued and supported in the school. Some of these steps require coordination so that responsibilities are shared. If, for example, you decide to increase the displays of student writing throughout the school, you may want to assign a different team for each month of the year, to ensure that student work is rotated routinely and writing is current.

➤ Every hallway in the school should have children's writing displayed not only at the eye level of adults but also at the eye level of children. It's important to remember, though, that the eye level of a kindergarten student is different from the eye level of a fourth grader. Some principals have had hanging strips installed at lower eye levels in the hallway to help with this. As students wait in line or transition from one class to another, they will have a ready source of reading material in front of them.

➤ Consider exhibiting writing in the cafeteria and in hallways outside the major resource rooms (gymnasium, art room, music room) as well. The writing should be mounted on construction paper or some colorful paper that draws attention to the displays.

➤ Classrooms should have book corners filled with trade books (both fiction and nonfiction), comfortable pillows and seating, as well as writing materials. In one school where one of the authors was a principal, an anonymous donor funded these book corners after the principal had spoken to a civic group about the importance of books in classrooms. Finding a source of funding these book corners can be a challenge, but the search may turn up some surprising results.

➤ The school office should have student work displayed so that visitors see it firsthand. Often, visitors never make it much further into the school than the office. Consider various ways that displays can be presented: on doors, on the front of counters, on bulletin boards, and near seating areas. Such displays say more about a school culture than any one person can convey.

➤ Be sure that there is plenty of reading material for children and adults in the office. Having comfortable chairs and tables filled with children's books, magazines, and original student books sends the message that this school takes literacy seriously. Consider asking each class to compile a collection of student writing into a book that can be shared in the office space.

➤ The principal's office should be accessible to the staff. Consider these questions: Are the doors open or closed? Do staff members feel comfortable walking into the principal's office to ask a question, share something positive, or share a concern? Where is the desk placed in the office? When students, staff, and parents come into the office, they should see evidence that the principal is a reader. Display children's literature visibly in addition to professional books.

➢ Look at all the areas of the school as potential places for books and other reading materials. The school clinic, for example, could have books for children to read as they are waiting for a parent to pick them up. The art classroom might display stories composed by students to accompany the display of art work. The physical education teacher might have students write directions for exercises and physical activities and post these on walls. And, of course, the principal's office itself should be replete with student work mounted and displayed on the walls.

Provide a Social and Affective Environment That Promotes Literacy

As mentioned earlier, the social and affective environment should promote a sense of community in which all members—students, staff, and parents—feel respected and valued. It is equally important to develop this positive environment around literacy experiences, so that each student, staff member, and parent knows that this is a school that values literacy. This value should be conveyed in all aspects and all places of the school day.

Principals and teachers should look for a variety of ways to use books and other reading material as a way to *celebrate the accomplishments* of all students. These celebrations do not need to be extensive or expensive.

➢ In a school where one of the authors was the principal, teachers identified one student in their classroom each week to be the "outstanding citizen" of the week. While the prior practice had been to give each citizen of the week an ice cream sandwich party, the principal (new to the school) decided to read a book to them instead. Over the course of the year (36 weeks), all children in the school had the opportunity to have this special time with the principal. As the children went back to their classrooms, they were given a small token (a pencil or a bookmark) and a letter that went home to their parents.

➢ Go into classrooms and read to students when they achieve something particularly noteworthy. For first graders, it might be the 100th day in school; for third graders, it might be learning the multiplication table; for fifth graders, it could be a social studies test they had all passed.

➢ Many schools have principal's challenges, where the principal encourages children to read a certain number of books. Once the students reach that mark (usually a relative high number), the principal agrees to do something special. Sometimes that something is unusual, such as sitting on the roof of the school or a dunking in the water booth at the school fair. Other times, though, the reward for students can be less daring. Students respond to a variety of activities.

➢ Consider holding an authors' conference to celebrate your students' writing. During an authors' conference, students throughout the school are given an opportunity to share a book they have written as well as engage in a variety of literacy activities throughout the day. They may, for example, make marbelized book covers in one activity while in another activity they may hear from a local writer.

➢ Hold a "book character" day during which students dress up as a character from one of the books they have read during the year. On that same day, community members can be invited into the school to share their favorite books with classes.

➢ Have a door-decorating contest for your offices and classes in which all doors are decorated as a book. At some point in the week, allow classes to view the decorated doors.

A positive affective environment is usually accompanied by a *collaborative environment* in which staff members feel they are part of a team and not just another "cog" in a wheel. More important, in a collaborative environment, staff members accept responsibility for the success of all students in their school, not just those in their class. In a collaborative environment, staff members work with each other on meaningful tasks (such as on the schoolwide committees mentioned earlier), have opportunities to participate in decision making, freely share ideas, resources, and supplies with fellow staff members, engage in professional networking outside of the school day, and view their school as a place of renewal or purpose. Often times, in this type of environment there is more risk taking and experimentation. In one school, teachers frequently received mini-grants from the local Chamber of Commerce because they were encouraged and supported for taking these risks.

These collaborative cultures do not happen without the leadership of the principal. The principal has to find ways to create time and a place for collaborative planning. The principal also must walk the talk by making decisions in a collaborative manner. Some ways to accomplish this include the following:

➢ Provide time during the day for committees to meet regularly. One principal provided this time on a quarterly basis and enlisted the help of retired teachers to cover classes while the committee members were in meetings. At another school, the grade level team arranged to cover the teacher's class while her committee meetings were held. There are countless ways time can be provided, if time is valued.

➢ Involve grade-level teams in student placements for the subsequent year. One principal held 2 days of meetings with grade-level teams to accomplish this. During each day, there were three 90-minute meetings: kindergarten, grade 1, and grade 2 teams, for example, met on day one; grade 3, grade 4, and grade 5 teams met on day 2. Four substitutes were hired for each day and rotated through each grade level while the teachers from that grade level were in the student placement meeting.

➢ Involve grade-level leaders in budget planning and budget choices. Many principals meet with grade-level leaders on a monthly basis. When it is time to submit the budget to the superintendent, these meetings can be instrumental in shaping the budget. As a result of this process, the principal may learn, for example, that more funds need to be set aside for purchase of "easy readers." Or the principal may decide that it is important to allocate each team a budget to use during the year.

➢ Involve staff in hiring decisions. Often times, there is a team approach for hiring administrators at the district level, but not at the school level. In one school, the principal interviewed teacher candidates with the literacy coach and two representatives from the grade-level team. The interviewers shared the hiring decision, and everyone then fully committed to helping that new teacher acclimate into the culture of the school. This same principal, by the way, also worked with her secretary and another secretary in the district to interview clerical help; she worked with the head of maintenance to interview for a custodial position.

Finally, an important part of strengthening the affective environment for literacy is to reinforce literacy through an informal network. All schools have an informal network in which ideas and information are shared. The more staff members are encouraged to share ideas and information about literacy in these networks, the more embedded literacy will become in the school culture. The principal can participate in and encourage this sharing of ideas by telling a staff member about a new idea for teaching reading or by letting a staff member know of a special workshop being offered in a neighboring school district.

Build an Academic Environment That Promotes Literacy Learning

As we've seen, committees can be an effective tool for promoting a positive affective climate. Marzano (2003) states, "Leadership for change is most effective when carried out by a small group of educators with the principal functioning as a strong cohesive force" (p. 174). Marzano is not alone in his belief that leadership must be inclusive, with shared responsibilities among staff members. Fullan (1995) and Senge (1990) note that the culture of the school changes when there is team work.

Involving staff members in decision making is a key element of many effective organizations. High-quality teams work more collaboratively and are more willing to propose risks. Roueche and Baker (1986) note that "Departmental, committee, and task force work are important ways that principals achieve excellent results."

Form a School Literacy Team

Cobb (2005) suggests that the implementation of *school literacy teams* provides a shared leadership vehicle for staff that can improve student literacy learning. Certainly the principal's role is critical in the formation of a school literacy team. The school literacy team generally consists of 10 to 12 staff members who represent the school population: classroom teachers, resource teachers, literacy coaches, media specialists, administrators, and other staff, such as teacher assistants. While teachers from every grade level do not need to be represented on the school literacy team, the team should include representative grade levels and/or subject area specialists in order to insure that planning is relevant for the entire school. Some schools have invited parents and other community members to serve on their team.

The team is led by the school principal. The team is tasked with reviewing multiple forms of school literacy data with the goal of identifying the needs of both students and staff. After reviewing the data, the team develops a list of students needing additional support as well as a plan for professional development for the staff. Finally, the team develops a list of recommendations to improve the literacy culture, presents it to the staff for feedback, modifies the recommendations, and then oversees the implementation of the recommendations.

In Chicago, for example, literacy teams provide up to 40 hours of staff development to subject area teachers and reading teachers. Through regular meetings, they are charged with establishing learning communities to discuss student work and literacy strategies.

Consider the Use of Literacy Coaches

Many schools and school districts have modified the roles of the reading specialist and/or Title I teacher to include literacy coaching. The International Reading Association (2004) has defined literacy coaching as something that provides "ongoing consistent support for the implementation and instruction components. It is nonthreatening and supportive. It gives a sense of how good professional development is. It also affords the opportunity to work with students." The role of the literacy coach has changed the reading specialist's role to one who focuses on meaningful professional development to support the school's literacy performance. For a more detailed discussion of literacy coaches, see Chapters 3 and 5.

Provide Large Blocks of Time for Literacy Instruction

Another major consideration for enhancing the academic climate for literacy is to organize the school schedule to ensure large blocks of time for literacy. Fountas and Pinnell (1996) emphasize the need for large blocked schedules for literacy instruction. There are a variety of ways to do this.

FOUR-BLOCKS MODEL One instructional model that provides larger blocks is the four-blocks model, which is a delivery system for teachers (Cunningham, Hall, & DeFee, 1998). The four blocks include a guided reading block, a self-selected reading block, a working-with-words block, and a writing block.

During the *guided reading* block, instruction is focused on comprehension. Children learn about typical story elements, such as character, setting, and plot. They also learn how to work with nonfiction text. All types of reading materials are used: big books, basal readers, magazines, trade books, and selections from science and social studies texts. The teacher may use whole-class, small-group, peer, and individual instruction during this block.

During the block called *working with words*, children learn to read and spell high-frequency words correctly by learning the word patterns. Through a variety of activities, teachers not only work with the entire group, they also monitor and assess the progress of individuals. Some of the planned activities include making words and word walls. For example, when students engage in a "making words" activity, they might use magnetic letters to change the beginning or ending of words.

The *self-selected reading* block provides all children with time for reading their own books as well as time for read-alouds. During this block, children choose what they want to read and teachers provide opportunity for them to respond to their reading in various settings. Often, individual conferences about the books are also held with children.

During the *writing block*, children write. They may be starting a new piece of writing, revising or editing a piece of writing, illustrating their writing, conferencing about their writing with the teacher, or putting the finishing touches on their writing. The teacher usually provides a mini-lesson on some common element that might appear in their writing. The mini-lesson also provides the children with a model for writing. An author's chair, a place where children share their own writing and respond to others' writing, is also frequently provided during this block.

PARALLEL BLOCK SCHEDULING Parallel block scheduling is a scheduling system that is used to help reduce the student–teacher ratio in core academic areas such as reading. Discussed by Canady and Rettig (1995), this schedule was developed as a way to prevent students from missing crucial instruction due to pull-outs.

Some of the benefits of parallel block scheduling include the size of the instructional group, reducing the interruptions for students during instruction, and providing more opportunities for individualized instruction. In this schedule, the teacher has fewer than 15 students at a time in his or her core reading block, and the remaining students in the class are scheduled for a resource period with a resource specialist in the school. One interesting finding of this schedule is that there is less disruptive behavior, primarily because there is less seatwork, during which children may be off task (Delaney, Toburen, Hooten, & Dozier, 1998).

As may be seen in Figure 2.3, Teachers A and B begin their class with an uninterrupted large block of time. During the next 50 minutes, Teacher A works with Group 1; Teacher B works with Group 3; and the extension teacher works with Group 2 and Group 4. Focused instruction could be a reading group, a writing workshop, or individual conferences with students. Since only half of the class is there at the time, the possibility of distractions is minimized.

In one school that used this scheduling, 2-hour blocks of literacy instruction were provided in the morning in grades K–2; grades 3–5 had their 2-hour block of literacy instruction in the afternoon. This 2-hour block allows the teacher to inte-

Teacher A	Large-group literacy (Groups 1 and 2)	Large-group literacy (Groups 1 and 2)	Focused instruction (Group 1)	Focused instruction (Group 2)
Teacher B	Large-group literacy (Groups 3 and 4)	Large-group literacy (Groups 3 and 4)	Focused instruction (Group 3)	Focused instruction (Group 4)
Teacher C	Focused instruction (Group 5)	Focused instruction (Group 6)	Large-group literacy (Groups 5 and 6)	Large-group literacy (Groups 5 and 6)
Teacher D	Focused instruction (Group 7)	Focused instruction (Group 8)	Large-group literacy (Groups 7 and 8)	Large-group literacy (Groups 7 and 8)
Extension Teacher	Focused instruction (Groups 6 and 8)	Focused instruction (Groups 5 and 7)	Focused instruction (Groups 2 and 4)	Focused instruction (Groups 1 and 3)

FIGURE 2.3. An example of a parallel block schedule.

grate reading and language arts and provide instruction that is deeper, as needed. During this 2-hour block, special education and other resource teachers were able to schedule their coteaching more effectively. More important, in a larger block of time, students had the opportunity to engage in authentic reading and writing activities.

Protect Instructional Time

Another important strategy a principal can use to ensure larger blocks of time is to ensure that *instructional time is uninterrupted*. One primary way principals can protect time is to decrease or eliminate announcements over the intercom system. Many schools allow announcements only during the first or last 5 minutes of school. Other strategies are varied and can include the following:

➢ Have a policy that does not allow noninstructional visitors to the classroom during teaching times.

➢ Do not schedule performances and other extracurricular activities during instructional time.

➢ Provide teachers with a sign for the door that lets drop-in visitors know when important literacy lessons are occurring. See Figure 2.4 for an example of what one principal used.

➢ Have your office staff screen all calls by saying, "Ms. Jones is teaching right now. May I take a message and have her call you when she is free?"

> *Our literacy time is short and stretched as far as it can be. Please leave a note so we do not lose any more time. Thanks!*

FIGURE 2.4. Sample sign for teachers' doors.

Provide Common Planning Time for Teachers in Each Grade

In order to provide a common planning time, principals need to create schedules that allow teachers within the same grade level to have the same noninstructional periods during which they can plan together. There are many ways this common planning time can be provided. Many schools provide it by ensuring that resource instruction, such as art, music, media, technology, and physical education, are provided at the same time to all students in a grade. Thus a team with four second-grade classrooms might have all their resource time at 1:00 P.M. each day, thereby providing classroom teachers with common planning time.

There are, however, other ways this time can be created. Whatever schedule is developed, teachers and staff must be involved in the decision-making process, as they are the ones most affected by the schedule.

- Resource teachers might agree, for example, to occasionally keep a group of students for two periods, allowing the teachers on the team to plan collaboratively for a longer period of time.
- Some schools have found that combining lunch time with a study hall or recess leads to a larger block of time for teachers. These schools often use parents to supervise this time, freeing up planning time for teachers.
- Some schools have scheduled their resource teachers for one day rather than throughout the week. In this model, second-grade classrooms would have a one full day of resource instruction a week with resource teachers, thus providing a full day of planning each week for classroom teachers.

Support Literacy in Every Area and throughout the Day

Supporting literacy in every curricular area throughout the day is known as "literacy across the curriculum." With this approach, students are learning literacy skills while learning other content, such as science, social studies, art, and music. The rationale for this approach is well explained by Moore, Moore, and Cunningham (2003). The key to ensuring that this instruction happens successfully is planning.

Specifically, teachers implementing literacy across the curriculum may have to be more flexible. For example, if they have an opportunity for writing in their science lesson, they may reduce writing time in the morning. In this approach, you may see books about math in the math center and books about science in the science center. It is not uncommon to see teachers making extensive use of children's literature in these areas. A third-grade classroom studying economics might have a bulletin board displaying important vocabulary such as *consumer, goods,* and *supplies*. Books in the center could include the *Berenstain Bears' Trouble with Money* by Stan and Jane Barenstain or Russell Hoban's *A Bargain for Francis*. A first-grade teacher studying seasonal climate changes might have books like *The Fall of Freddie the Leaf* by Leo Buscaglia, a story about the life cycle of a leaf.

Build the Supply of Trade Books, Both Fiction and Nonfiction, in Your School

The availability of books in your school is essential in order to develop an academic culture that enhances literacy. Books should be everywhere: in classrooms, in offices, on desks, and in common areas. Children's ready access to books will pay off when you see them walking in the school with a book in their hand, so enrapt in the story that they cannot put the book down.

Every classroom should have an extensive classroom library. As mentioned earlier, one of us received an anonymous donation from a community member to supply our book corners. Other sources can be found through mini-grants from the local Chamber of Commerce or through parent donations.

Support Professional Development

As a principal, you are responsible for your staff members' professional growth. How you approach this area is critical to your school's academic environment. Professional development should not be something that is done *to* teachers but something that is done *with* teachers. Staff development is best when it is planned collaboratively with teachers and when there is a provision of ongoing support and resources.

How you and your staff decide to approach staff development is important. Some of the best staff development in literacy will do the following:

- Respect the capacity of teachers and principals
- Reflect best research practices
- Enable teachers to develop further expertise in literacy strategies, content, and technologies
- Require substantial allocation of time and other resources

Principals must find time for staff development and be creative and flexible in their approach. Here are some possibilities for finding time:

➤ *Modify the school calendar* to periodically release students early so that teachers can participate in professional development activities during the regular school day. Some schools, for example, have an early-release day on one Wednesday a quarter. The daily schedule on the remaining days is adjusted to compensate for the time students are not in school.

➤ *Use a common group of substitutes on a regular basis.* Some principals may bring in four substitutes for 2 days in order to provide over an hour of release time for each team (see Figure 2.5).

➤ *Use common planning time* to allow for professional development during the school day.

When developing plans for staff development, there are alternatives that should be considered to the simple one-shot workshop.

➤ *Action-based research* requires teachers to design and pursue investigations. By collecting and analyzing data, teachers gain insights that can change their classroom practices. In an action-based research, teachers share the results with colleagues.

➤ *School visits* are an excellent way for staff members to learn a new approach or strategy. Tremendous learning occurs when teachers and staff members view the implementation of a new approach firsthand. Staff members at the host school will offer a different perspective if they have been using the strategy for a while. School visits should also provide time for the visiting staff members to ask questions and discuss what they have observed.

➤ *Peer coaching* is a strategy that can provide one-to-one assistance to teachers. The relationship is developed through common planning of lessons, classroom

Day One	**9:30-11:00**	**11:00-12:30**	**1:00-2:30**
Substitute One	Grade 1 - A	Grade 2 - A	Grade K - A
Substitute Two	Grade 1 - B	Grade 2 - B	Grade K - B
Substitute Three	Grade 1 - C	Grade 2 - C	Grade K - C
Substitute Four	Grade 1 - D	Grade 2 - D	Grade K- D
Day Two			
Substitute One	Grade 3 - A	Grade 4 - A	Grade 5 - A
Substitute Two	Grade 3 - B	Grade 4 - B	Grade 5 - B
Substitute Three	Grade 3 - C	Grade 4 - C	Grade 5 - C
Substitute Four	Grade 31 - D	Grade 4 - D	Grade 5 - D

FIGURE 2.5. The use of four substitutes during the school day.

observations, joint development of materials, and strategizing to meet students' needs. Joyce and Showers (1996) report that the act of observing another teacher is a powerful professional development experience, regardless of whether there is verbal feedback.

➢ *Study groups* can be organized around a particular topic. A group of teachers might want to learn more about reading workshop. They would gather books and materials to read and discuss their reading in a study group. Leadership for the group can be rotated or assigned to one individual. In addition to reading and discussing current literature about the topic, study groups typically visit other school sites and attend conferences or classes to gather additional information.

➢ *Staff retreats* are often held at the beginning of the year. An uninterrupted session allows staff the time to develop goals and plans strategies based on their needs. In addition, staff morale is often boosted by these sessions, as is the sense of a learning community.

More information about professional development is contained in Chapter 3.

Spread Enthusiasm for the Community of Learners within the Larger Community

Visitors can sense when there is a community of learners within a school. The climate is palpable, with evidence from many sources visible in the school. A school that has a positive academic climate shares its values and experiences with visitors who come into the school:

➢ Ask visitors to write down their favorite book as they sign in. Later, classes can graph the favorite books of visitors to the school.

➢ Have a staff bulletin board that shows a photograph of each staff member reading their favorite book.

➢ Consider a student bulletin board showing photographs of students reading their favorite books.

➢ In one school that participated in a local United Way campaign, the organizer held a lottery for those who had contributed to the campaign. Lottery prizes included a variety of professional books and were awarded in random drawings. These drawings were conducted when community members from the United Way were present.

➢ Hold a "Good-bye Book" day during which the oldest students in your school say good-bye to their favorite books by reading them with the younger students in your school.

➢ Hold elections for the favorite book of the semester. The elections can be organized by grade level groups (kindergarten and first grade, second and third grades, fourth and fifth grades), with the results shared on an informative bulletin board.

CONCLUSIONS

The discussion of school culture and school climate in this chapter has emphasized four important aspects: the physical environment, the social environment, the affective environment, and the academic environment. After a general discussion about these four aspects, we described in detail suggestions for building a culture of literacy. Several ways to create a physical environment that supports literacy were discussed, including the importance of student work displayed at eye level and ample books and reading material throughout the school. Ways to create a social and affective environment to support literacy included a variety of recognition programs, schoolwide celebrations, and the establishment of a collaborative culture. Finally, the academic environment was discussed, with the need for principal leadership paramount.

LOOKING AHEAD

The culture in your school communicates to everyone in your community: students, staff, parents, and community members. As you attend to the culture, the need for professional development will become paramount. By offering quality professional development, a school principal can begin to change the culture significantly. Our next chapter will focus how to build a professional development program that supports literacy.

CHAPTER 3

BUILDING A PROFESSIONAL DEVELOPMENT PROGRAM

An Essential for Success

DAVID GASTON

> Every system is designed to produce the results it gets.
>
> —SPARKS (2002)

The many duties that principals must perform on a daily basis are mind boggling. Between disciplinary cases, administrative duties, classroom observations, faculty meetings, community programs, and parent meetings, it is a wonder that a principal can provide meaningful instructional leadership.

The increased pressure of NCLB standards and various state accountability programs places an additional layer of stress and strain on any principal's shoulders. Many days, clarity and purpose in the principal's work seem to fall by the wayside as the building administrator suddenly crawls out of his or her rabbit hole, only to discover that it is 5:00 or 6:00 P.M. and he or she has accomplished little

David Gaston, EdD, is the principal at Berkeley Middle School in Williamsburg, Virginia. He recently served as an elementary principal. Dr. Gaston has worked as a classroom teacher, a central office administrator, and a building administrator at the elementary, middle, and high school levels. In addition, he has been an adjunct faculty member at Old Dominion University and the College of William and Mary, where he teaches graduate-level courses in curriculum and instruction. His work in education has also extended to training and consulting with the International Baccalaureate Primary Years Programme across North America and the Caribbean.

in the line of what would be deemed meaningful work. All principals have found themselves here at many points in their careers.

Despite the daily demands on the principal, the role of a principal as a change agent in a learning community cannot be ignored. On many days when they might find themselves caught in the endless maze of managerial and operational duties, principals must remind themselves of the one role that is central to everything—*their ability to facilitate and sustain meaningful change in their schools as instructional leaders* (DuFour & Berkey, 1995). From the moment that they enter their building—whether as a neophyte principal or a veteran on the force – their ability to bring about change to help all of their students achieve academic success must remain their driving focus.

Notice how the emphasis remains focused on *supporting student achievement*. It is all about the students in the classrooms. As principals, it is the ability to facilitate and enhance student success, especially through relationships with teachers, that will bring about the greatest and most sustainable achievement within the school. Teachers should wish to engage and excite students in their classroom and encourage them to be learners. Principals should desire to engage, excite, and support their teachers to allow them to produce these great student performances (Schlechty, 2002).

How can a principal support his or her teachers in this endeavor? First and foremost, the principal—as the primary instructional leaders in the learning community, must build and sustain a culture that establishes, supports, and remains committed to quality professional development. In the end, the ultimate worth of any professional development program will be the vital role that it plays in improving student performance (Cook & Fine, 1997a).

RATIONALE FOR PROFESSIONAL DEVELOPMENT

While the research that documents the best approaches to build and sustain teacher expertise is limited, there is significant evidence that professional development, *particularly in the area of reading*, can have a positive effect on teaching and produces significantly higher results in student achievement (Learning First Alliance, 2000; Fielding, Kerr, & Rosier, 2007). A systematic program of professional development must be embedded throughout the entire structure and culture of the school—a bottom to top, top to bottom system that embraces the entire workplace (DuFour & Berkey, 1995).

The specific challenge to schools is increased student achievement in the areas of reading and mathematics, as specified in NCLB. These accountability standards demand that every child read at or on grade level by the year 2014. Because of these requirements, the already critical value of reading instruction is placed on an even higher level in our schools.

The standardized tests of achievement developed at the state level must be read and comprehended by students in order for them to be able to engage and apply the content. Obviously, these tests demand a certain level of essential student knowledge in the content area; however, every child also needs to be able to read and comprehend the questions that are placed before them at test time. Simply put—if they can't read the test, they won't be able to successfully pass the test. Knowing how to read and comprehend the test will allow our students to find the greatest chances of reaching success.

Additionally, and more importantly, it is our most challenging, and enormous, responsibility as educators to teach our children to read. The gift of literacy remains the single most important common thread to instruction at every level. Teacher performances, especially at the elementary level, should focus around instruction that weaves literacy into every aspect of our daily instruction. Teachers must know how best to teach literacy at all instructional levels with a toolbag that allows them to skillfully and masterfully teach each child.

Literacy skills remain the most important element and determiner of students' success in their academic careers. Although the research that documents the best way to design a professional development program to build teacher expertise in literacy is limited, the Learning First Alliance (2000) states that there is significant evidence that professional development in reading will produce positive effects on teaching and will produce significantly higher student achievement.

The Learning First Alliance states that "central in the discussion of school improvement is the belief, supported by research, that almost all students can learn to read and that much reading failure is preventable" (Learning First Alliance, 2000, p. 2). In this context, reading becomes not just one major area of focus, but *the* major area of focus for principals to support through a program of sustained and ongoing professional development within their learning communities.

Teachers need continuous and focused training to prevent students from becoming members of the ranks of those adolescents who struggle to read. If a student is not reading at grade level by the third grade, the risks of academic difficulty increase significantly. A comprehensive program of professional development that provides teachers with the skills needed to successfully negotiate early literacy skills during the primary years, as well as fluency and comprehension skills in the later elementary years, will give teachers the tools they need.

Teacher expertise and effectiveness is one of the most important variables that affects student achievement, and quality teaching can only be developed, supported, and sustained by school leaders who establish thoughtful, research-based, systematic programs of professional development for their frontline instructors (Darling-Hammond, 1997; Sparks, 2002).

Reading Focus

Learning to read is at the core of every school. It is what parents expect and what children must learn to do well to succeed in school and in life. The challenge for teachers is how to unlock the reading code for students, often 20–25 at a time.

These young people enter school with a wide range of ability levels and varying degrees of reading readiness. This daunting task was made more manageable with the implementation of the readers' workshop model. Our reading specialist and a first grade teacher began this new approach to their instruction by working collaboratively and gradually inviting other staff in to watch their lessons.

In a nutshell, the students gather around the teacher who introduces a topic using a story or book—for example, if the objective is to teach characterization. The selection read highlights strong characterization, and how authors establish characterization is discussed, modeled, and shared. Students then go to their "book nook" (their favorite reading spot) to read. The teacher then circulates to individual children while they read and examine different books for characterization. When circulating, the teacher monitors and supports student understanding of the objective.

This model requires a lot of planning and pacing, but it is worth it. Lost to the students is the old "red bird, blue bird" group where slower students felt intimidated by more advanced readers. It is amazing to watch the depth of knowledge and understanding that is created through reader's workshop.

This approach was shared, modeled, and supported by our school staff. It gradually spread and became an integral part of the instructional program. The great thing is that it works!

Lucia Villa Sebastian, EdD
Chief Academic Officer, York County School Division

DEVELOPING THE FOUNDATION

Designing, instituting, monitoring, and evaluating a comprehensive professional development program in literacy instruction is a daunting task for any principal that requires the participation of the entire learning community. Literacy and reading instruction weaves itself into every facet of student learning.

Determine Your Resources

One of the best places to begin with any broad and ambitious staff development initiative is to determine the human resources within the school community. It would seem obvious that the teachers would be the main focus of a professional development program. The learning community, however, also includes parents, business partners, central office support personnel, school support staff such as reading specialists, media specialists, Reading Recovery specialists, and student mentors, and, of course, the students themselves.

All stakeholders in the learning community should be consulted when developing a professional development program (DuFour & Eacker, 1998). Senge's (1990) work, which focuses on the interrelationships between systems during change, sees the involvement of these stakeholders as imperative, for any of these individuals or groups could, at any time, dramatically affect another stakeholder within the system through their actions or decisions. A sustained and systematic program of professional development will need to involve the entire array of people who are responsible for its success.

Look Outside the School for Support

As the principal begins looking at the broader picture of professional development, time will be a major factor that will either contribute to its success or doom the program to failure. In order to open the possibility of more time during the instructional day for professional development devoted to literacy instruction, district personnel should be consulted to determine whether or not such changes will affect teacher contract hours or get the school into difficulty with any of the unions or teacher associations. Including the local educational association or union representative on the professional development team is strongly suggested in these cases. Negotiating this potential minefield is critical to success, especially in states that have a strong union presence.

Consult Support Staff

Support staff can also be affected when scheduling professional development. Often, paraprofessionals and other support staff interact with students on tightly-constructed and constrained schedules and should be involved as stakeholders in any larger conversation that focuses on professional development. Additionally, consideration should be given in this process to any possibility that the role of the specialist or paraprofessional might change. The position of the reading specialist might change, for example, if he or she is asked to become more of a reading coach to teachers and less of a reading tutor for students. Staff need an early understanding that this kind of change might be on the way, and it is important to develop ways to embrace this change, prepare for the change, and work with any shifting paradigms that it may bring.

Don't Forget Parents

Parents should be allowed to participate and offer input into how they might be able to support a professional development program that may change the way their children are being instructed in reading. Through this inclusion and ownership, parents can gain valuable insight and understanding into the overall benefits for their children when their school undertakes an effective and focused professional development program.

It is vital to be sure to include a representation of all stakeholders in the exploration and brainstorming processes and meetings related to literacy instruction at the school. All of these groups could adversely affect the change process if they are not consulted and included. Through building a strong network of input and insight, the program of professional development will gain strength and vitality as well as a sure foothold at its inception.

Review the Current Research

Another important foundation for a sustained professional development effort is the identification of the current and pertinent research. Comparing current instructional approaches and curriculum with the research is the optimal place to begin the process (Abouzeid, 2006). Research-based instructional strategies that support teaching and learning are essential in this age of accountability and cannot be ignored in the construction of a program for a sustained and successful professional development program in literacy (Abouzeid, 2006).

Once the pertinent research has been identified, a thorough review will be an important next step. Studies should focus on information and findings that parallel or match the specific school's current profile, including demographic information, performance indicators, assessment data and results, evaluation tools, instructional methodologies, and current programs.

DuPree (1989) advocates embarking on a thorough assessment of one's current reality before delving deeper into the problem-solving stages. Exploring the school's current achievement data and information to determine broader areas of feasibility, sustainability, budgets, breadth of support, and program capacity will be vitally important in determining where the principal and staff members find themselves at present and where they would like to go in the future. Student achievement data, for example, will provide insight into the depth of need for student remediation and the type of programmatic changes and training that the staff will require to support the desired change. Budget information will determine the difference between hiring outside consultants or providing internal programming to keep costs under control.

Build Consensus

Perhaps the most challenging part of developing a comprehensive program of professional development lies in consensus building. Teachers, parents, students, paraprofessionals, business and community leaders, administrators, mentors, and tutors—the entire learning community—should be involved in the initial discussions about the program. Most schools and their districts may have a professional development program to which the district has subscribed or established in its routine practice. Each individual school, however, is unique, with different demographic data and different community expectations. These differences may require the school community to further explore what will work within their own instructional practice and programming.

The consensus-building process is a vital information-gathering stage that seeks to take in all of the different parts and approaches to the literacy program in an effort to determine the direction that the program will need to take. Gaffney, Hesbol, and Corso (2005) likened the consensus-building process to any learning process for any individual. If, for example, one wanted to learn more about a particular form of exercise, he or she would likely turn to all of the information available on that program—from friends to DVDs to books and gyms—in an effort to get their opinions on that particular exercise program (Gaffney, et. al., 2005). Likewise, as a principal embarks on the journey of building a sustainable program for literacy, he or she will need to gather information from many sources to determine individual and community need, the faculty's ability to sustain and support such a program, the community's ability to understand and support the program, and the student data that will drive much of the program.

This is a great time to get clear information regarding everyone's desires, hopes, and visions for the program and to learn about individual and collective contributions that might be important to the program. Principals tend to have a feeling that they must know everything about every possible topic related to education and instruction. This generalist attitude and approach must be broken in an effort to move into the role of a community facilitator—a learning leader—in which the principal can gain an understanding of areas outside their expertise through others who can guide, assist, and mentor them.

Beginning the Consensus Process

Consensus building can take place in exploratory sessions and meetings, where objectives and goals are identified, priorities are established, research is reviewed, required materials and assistance are identified, and the effectiveness of the program will be determined. Other suggestions for building consensus within the learning community include the following

- Focus groups that explore needs and considerations
- Informal principal teas or coffee hours to talk to cross-sections of the community about literacy instruction and various needs to support the program
- Community chat nights at various convenient off-campus sites where dialogue and discussion about the literacy needs of the students can freely and openly take place

In many cases, these consensus-building processes can uncover a wealth of community resources, such as a local college or university or fiscal underwriting from local business partners, which can assist in supporting a powerful professional development program.

Information Gathering

Hall and Horde (2001) suggest two practical methods for seeking input and building consensus. One method is what they term the *one-legged conferencing* method, where brief conversations between colleagues take place in the hallways, cafeteria, playgrounds, and during unstructured time. Another more formal approach to information gathering consists of an *open-ended statement of concern*, where the principal presents various questions about approaches to, in this case, literacy and then receives written responses to the questions (Hall & Horde, 2001). These responses can be analyzed and reviewed on a continuum in an effort to get an idea of the school's literacy program and its development.

Both of these techniques can successfully blend to produce solid consensus among all of the stakeholders. Informally, talking with individuals and small groups of colleagues and parents about the direction for a literacy program and how they would like to see it structured is a great way to gather informal and honest feedback. It also presents a powerful approach to building program capacity and generating enthusiasm for the program in anticipation of the change that such a program can bring.

Role of the School Literacy Team

At faculty meetings, members of a school literacy team can make formal presentations to the faculty regarding aspects of a comprehensive literacy program, which can include elements such as reported student Title I data. Using this information as a springboard for discussion, questions and answers posed throughout the meeting can bring to life new ideas and uncover new information or "a-ha's." These ideas can then be incorporated into building agreement as to specific faculty needs in the area of reading instruction. A sharp and surgical focus on the data can provide great insight into the specific professional strengths and areas of need within a faculty regarding reading instruction.

This data paves the way for an open and honest conversation within the school community that needs to take place without the assignment of blame to individuals, grade-level teams, or support teams. It should involve all members of the faculty and staff in an effort to tease out every possible angle, explanation, and challenge that is implied with the reading data. These conversations—while at times either difficult or sobering—can allow the faculty to move toward developing a needs assessment. This is vital to the development of a comprehensive professional development program in literacy. Only through the analysis of our successes and shortcomings can the administration, the teachers, and the entire learning community begin to truly understand where the seeds of continuous improvement need to be planted.

Conduct a Needs Assessment

A needs assessment is an important tool that determines what strengths and shortfalls exist within the learning community. For teachers, the needs assessment will focus on their strengths and needs regarding instructional strategies and classroom practices. A needs assessment can also assist in determining which faculty members may be strong in-house resources that can be tapped for mentoring or coaching positions. It may also determine which individuals will require additional support in a variety of fields and thus build a more complete landscape for the comprehensive professional development program required to provide that support to them.

The needs assessment should consist of questions that determine what is needed to create a strong reading program in the building. Additionally, the faculty should be prompted to provide focused feedback on the areas of instruction in which they require additional training to become stronger teachers of reading (see Figure 3.1).

Finally, and most important, the needs assessment should focus on the strengths and needs most important for the principal to understand. Questions should be designed to determine what resources the principal will need to harness to support the faculty and staff. Other questions should help hone the principal's focus on the school's current reading data. The provocations within the needs assessment should also focus in large part on a wide range of ability and instructional styles among the faculty. In this way, the principal will be capable of tapping into the existing strengths of their faculty to determine whether further training and assistance is required to enhance the reading program and to identify areas of deficit where training and development are required.

This last idea is vitally important to the success of the program, as the school community must be able to see and understand that support for this program comes from an individual who recognizes his or her own needs and strengths. The principal must be willing to train and develop alongside all of the other stakeholders in the learning community in order to enhance the community's buy-in and desire to participate in the professional development program. Presence and participation is a non-negotiable for the principal in any program of professional development. A principal cannot ask for the faculty, staff, and stakeholders to get excited about and participate in a program of sustained professional development if these individuals do not see the leadership both present and enthusiastic about the training that is offered.

In all efforts given toward building a comprehensive professional development program in support of reading instruction, principals must, as instructional leaders, convey their passion for continuous professional development and the positive growth opportunity that such an experience offers to the entire learning community. DuFour and Berkey (1995) state this ideal best:

> Principals who pursue training opportunities, participate in study groups, forward articles to staff members and solicit their comments, make presentations at conferences, write articles for professional journals, and engage in action research at the school site are using their own behavior to communicate the importance of professional growth. They are mindful of Ralph Waldo Emerson's admonition that what we do thunders above us so loudly that others cannot hear what we say. (p. 4)

Team/Grade Level (Name is Optional): ____________________

I AM/WE ARE:

- Comfortable and knowledgeable about phonemic awareness

  Strongly agree Agree Disagree Strongly Disagree

Comments: ____________________

____

- Knowledgeable about teaching students how to read fluently with phrasing and accuracy

  Strongly agree Agree Disagree Strongly Disagree

Comments: ____________________

____

- Comfortable teaching comprehension strategies to my students

  Strongly agree Agree Disagree Strongly Disagree

Comments: ____________________

____

- Most pleased with my students' progress in writing in the following areas:

  Strongly agree Agree Disagree Strongly Disagree

Comments: ____________________

____

- Comfortable with the current word study/spelling program

  Strongly agree Agree Disagree Strongly Disagree

Comments: ____________________

____

- Interested in participating in professional development:

  Strongly agree Agree Disagree Strongly Disagree

Comments: ____________________

____

Thank you for your participation and feedback!

FIGURE 3.1. School Literacy Team Survey for Professional Development.

KEY ELEMENTS OF A PROFESSIONAL DEVELOPMENT PROGRAM

The data gleaned and collected from a well-developed needs assessment will provide a gold mine of information about the faculty when it comes to reading instruction. The data will reveal universal areas of need and required training from which the entire faculty will benefit.

Provide for Individual Differences

While some areas of need are universal, principals must recognize that there will be more specific areas of the data that reveal the needs of smaller groups and/or individuals. These smaller groups and/or individuals will require very specific training to help them move to another level. Paramount to building this program is the sobering truth that not everyone will be in the same place in terms of their instructional ability and prior knowledge and practice in literacy. This means that any program must offer meaningful training for the beginner who is just starting to wade through the literacy program as well as the veteran who wishes to hone his or her skills so the most recently validated strategies can be put into practice.

Teachers must approach literacy instruction from a solidly balanced approach that demands from them an ability to understand, recognize, and work with each individual student in their classroom. Every faculty member will not have the same ability levels and strengths in the areas that their students require. They will demand an extensive menu of development experiences and then require consistent follow-up and mentoring experiences to solidify their development in literacy instruction.

Just as students' entering behaviors and levels of understanding require teachers to build background knowledge in their students, the same can and should be assumed with your faculty and support staff. Chances are they did not have similar courses in their preparatory training that covered literacy instruction. The tools and practices that they bring with them from their college and university training may represent vastly different avenues, approaches, and exposures. All of these will have to be strengthened in order to allow faculty and staff to effectively deliver such instruction. Building background knowledge of literacy instruction is just as important for faculty as building background knowledge is to students.

A strong staff development program will allow everyone to start their training at their own individual level, much as we do with individual students. If, for example, a teacher needs help with guided reading, there may be individual teachers in the building who can serve as model teachers for training. A good place to start would be to allow peer observers to visit a master teacher's classroom during a guided reading lesson and debrief on the experience. Principals could use their substitute budget—or grant money that might be available to pay substitute teachers—to cover multiple classes. If a principal has a limited budget, internal coverage could be arranged by a reading specialist or coach, the Title I teacher, or even the principal or assistant principal if they are so inclined. Remember, in order to be strong leaders for learning, principals have to be learners themselves.

Find Time for Professional Development

Determining the best time to offer professional development programs will also be a key factor in setting the stage for success. Teacher planning time is sacred and often difficult to negotiate for any meeting time, particularly for any professional development modules, considering the myriad tasks that a teacher must cram into these short, daily periods. Additionally, team planning and dialogue must be maintained to support the professional learning community. If teachers opt for cohort training during planning time once per week, however, a trainer can use this time to teach, mentor, practice, and discuss the elements of their craft.

As a principal, developing many different opportunities for training can be absolutely daunting and exhausting. At many points, there might be two, three, or even four separate trainings occurring in the same week—sometimes simultaneously. During the day, the reading specialist or coach could be in targeted classrooms working with teachers in developing a reading and writing workshop approach or working with newly adopted basal and its supplemental texts. In the same day or week, teachers could be conducting peer observations to sharpen their organizational and instructional skills in their own classrooms. Later in the week, the Title I specialist could be working with teachers on writing modules that incorporate state writing standards and the writing rubric that supports these standards in an effort to sharpen students' writing skills in identified need areas. Additionally, there might be an afternoon or evening book study with a small group of interested teachers. Finally, teacher teams could gather together during a planning period to review data and discuss professional literature that supports the school's literacy approach. This literature, of course, would have been read and reviewed prior to the meeting in an effort to provide a springboard for meaningful dialogue and discussion within the teacher team. This would be ongoing through the semester or the school year.

Since the professional development experiences that the school is establishing are to be lasting and meaningful, certain *ground rules or agreements* will need to be established within the faculty family. First, no matter what must be done in education, there will never be enough time to meet the demands in the course of each day or year. The challenge becomes to review the current structures and to build time both after and before school in order to find time within the day for such experiences as peer observation and coaching, which that are vitally important to the success of the reading program.

Examine the School's Master Schedule

A school's master schedule can severely hamstring efforts at building a professional development program in literacy. Providing common planning and professional development time is often hampered by a school schedule that is disjointed and erratic. Discussions with school leaders that focus on these schedules produce frustration, because many times the cause of this dysfunctional schedule includes outside factors that are beyond the administrator's control, such as budgets that can only support itinerant teachers, split grade levels, low to dwindling student populations, or formal or informal leadership within the building that has established the master schedule and maintained it for years.

Whatever the case might be, providing continuous, protected, common planning time to teachers will be paramount in allowing them to plan and practice their new learning from the professional development program. If there is, for example, difficulty in establishing common planning time among grade levels and support specialists, a modified parallel block schedule (see Chapter 2) or A/B rotation schedule needs to be explored and considered as part of a larger effort to support the professional development program.

If it is not possible to modify the school day schedule, constructing monthly after-school planning sessions that can be forums for professional development may also be considered. Additionally, evening or Saturday sessions can be successful—especially if you have the event catered or provide some great food to support the faculty—with the right planning and investigation. Conducting training at an off-site location should also be a serious consideration, as it will enhance in teachers the feeling of being treated like a professional.

Finally, principals should consider providing full or half days of release time that can be funded with state remediation money, grant money, or even district funding. Gathering teacher teams at an off-site location for a half or full day of planning or training once or twice a year will be productive and fun and can reap some amazing results. Obviously, some of these considerations need to be given serious review and consultation—especially with the stakeholders and even union leaders, if this is to be successful.

Cook and Fine (1997b) share that the "reality is that teachers likely will require *more* than 20% of their work time for learning and collaboration if they are to be successful in implementing ambitious reform initiatives" (p. 3). The principal and the planning team must help teachers find the time to ensure that the professional development becomes a part of the schedule and expectation for the day, not just delivered outside of the instructional day.

As tiring as all of this may seem, this dynamic approach to learning and study is driven through the common belief that the entire learning community can work together to meet one another's needs and bring continuous and meaningful professional development in reading to the school.

Develop a Budget

Budget will certainly be a major consideration in building a continuous professional development program in reading instruction. How the principal funds the professional development program can run the gamut from creative to straightforward, depending on the individual school district, the availability of federal and local dollars, and grant availability. Title I funds, for example, are often strictly guarded and it is predetermined as to where they can and cannot be spent. A strong Title I leader at the school district level, along with creative Title I specialists at the building level know that these funds can go a long way toward supporting a sustained program of professional development in reading. Many times, Title I funds can bring specialized help and materials that benefit all the staff when there is a collaborative culture.

Additionally, grant funds can be used to provide training over a concentrated period of time. Grant funds present a challenge on many occasions when used to fund any educational program. The learning community or school district writes the grant, extends painstaking energy to get it tailored to support a specific program, celebrates the grant when it is finally awarded, builds the professional development program in reading, and two or three years down the road, watches as the program then has to disappear because there was no capacity built into the plan to sustain the program after the grant expires. Grants are great, but it must be pointed out that at some point—usually sooner than later—the money will go away and will have to be replaced by a permanent funding stream that will sustain the capacity for change. The leadership and stakeholder team will have to project a long-term budget in the planning stages, especially if the program that is riding on the grant funding becomes a permanent fixture in the building's overall program.

On the flip side, however, grant funding can provide a temporary injection of dollars to fund a powerful and concentrated program of professional development, especially if the monitoring and continuous practice capacities are anticipated and built into a more permanent funding formula. Grants are useful in funding train-the-trainer programs or in providing a generalized training program with outside consultants over 2 or 3 years. However, if either of these approaches is employed, it must be given long-term support as a permanent part of the professional development program through continuous internal monitoring and advanced training among key "experts" within the building who can carry the momentum forward.

In this age of accountability, most states offer remediation money that can also be used to fund professional development programs in reading. As mentioned earlier, reading is fundamental to all accountability testing—if students cannot read the test, they will not pass the test. Most state accountability and remediation program money does not come with strings that tell principals and districts how that money can and should be spent. While most of that money more often than not winds up funding after-school remediation programs, most of these programs focus on literacy and numeracy. Using these dollars for literacy supplies and training among the teaching staff as part of the remediation efforts at the school can be a smart way to build long-term capacity among the staff in reading development, as well as increasing student achievement.

Case Study 1. Using Title I Money to Fund Literacy Training

> One Targeted-Assisted Title I school was faced with an increasing number of half-day kindergarten students who did not have any preschool literacy exposure. Consequently, as the school continued to monitor their data, they found that the students possessed tremendous gaps in their development of letter recognition and phonemic awareness. In an effort to offer acceleration to the students and as a way to bring training and consistency to the kindergarten team of teachers, the learning community prepared a written proposal to the district office to use their Title I money to fund a part-time specialist for kindergarten who had extensive training in Fountas and Pinnell's work in preliteracy skills.
>
> The proposal identified the major role that this individual would play. The specialist would work closely with the half-day kindergarten team to pull out students for small-group and one-to-one remediation. The specialist would train the kindergarten teacher team in the techniques used in the pull-out sessions so the techniques would translate consistently into the classroom. The specialist would also meet and confer with parents to provide them with materials and training for student support at home.

This proposal was certainly a risk. The students would be measured using a specific assessment—the Phonemic Awareness Literacy Screening (PALS). This would be the only single measure of success for these kindergarten students. Supporting data was incorporated into the proposal, but this data could not be counted, as the other schools within the district were not using the same measures. In the end, the kindergarten teacher team used this single year of experience to further student achievement in preliteracy skills, develop their own repertoires in how best to instruct to the various needs of their students, and encourage parent connections and participation in assisting their young readers to find success. At the end of the school year, the students showed strong, statistically significant gains in preliteracy skills, per the PALS measure, with every student at or above the cut scores for literacy success. The additional data that was collected was also examined, and, although it couldn't be compared with that of the sister elementary schools, the data showed significant growth among the earliest readers at the school.

Early identification and remediation offered the team a chance to increase their knowledge and unify around a common approach to literacy that helped them find greater accountability and achievement. Because of the success of the program, the first-grade team of teachers was able to take their students further in their journey to literacy the following year. The kindergarten specialist whose position was funded in the original proposal was hired as a full-time teacher on the kindergarten team which continued to assist the kindergarten teachers by allowing for a much smaller class size. In an effort to continue with professional development, these teachers worked with their first-grade colleagues to train them in the strategies and approaches that they used in their kindergarten classrooms. They also assisted in team planning and collaboration to support student transition from kindergarten to first grade as students matriculated to their next grade level. These collaborative combined planning sessions allowed the kindergarten and first grade teachers the opportunity to review individual student data, vdetermine student need, and prepare students as they moved to the next grade level. Everyone came out a winner in this case, and the experience strengthened student skills and teacher collegiality as the professional development program unfolded.

Case Study 2. Using Grant Money to Fund Team Planning

An elementary school had reading teachers who were very interested in expanding their conversation and planning capacity regarding literacy and reading instruction practice in their classrooms. The faculty agreed to use state assessment grant money to fund substitute teachers for two release days during the school year. The purpose of these release days would be to allow for concentrated and uninterrupted grade-level team planning to discuss student progress, review and select literature for upcoming units, reflect on reading units and assessments, and discuss data and classroom approaches in an effort to enhance student reading performance. On these days, each grade-level team was encouraged to meet off-site in a relaxed atmosphere with all of their data and materials for discussion. Also, during this time, if any additional teacher training was required, the team would notify knowledgeable colleagues to plan and schedule professional development time when they returned to school.

These planning days were a huge hit with the entire faculty in the sense that they built internal capacity for dialogue and training, strengthened the team approach to planning within the professional learning community, and identified more areas of need through the collective exchange of ideas. Teams would identify elements upon which they might require further training and would bring these elements back to the school literacy team and administration for future reference in the program of continuous development.

Capitalize on the Talents and Expertise of Staff Members

It must be understood that everyone on the school's faculty will be at very different levels of experience in reading instruction. Some will know how to lead a guided reading group expertly and will have a structure and rhythm in place in their classrooms that is evident every time you step foot in their classroom door. Others will be able to work well with assessment data, administering cloze passages, read and retells, or other diagnostic instruments to students and then using this data to discern in their instruction the best path toward student success. Yet others will have an incredible depth of knowledge when it comes to phonics and phonemic awareness and will know various tools and approaches that lend themselves wonderfully to success with their younger students.

These experts need to be recognized, celebrated, and encouraged to lead in the professional development that takes place in the building. They should also be encouraged to share their knowledge with the volunteers and parents who spend time with students; this will help maintain consistency and will support students outside of the classroom.

In addition, if the principal has expertise in a particular field that is identified from the needs assessment, he or she should take this opportunity to offer training. It should be cautioned, however, that the principal should also participate in other sessions that are offered, not just the session they provide. Any principal or administrator should carefully gauge the staff members' receptiveness to having him or her serve as a literacy trainer or coach for a specific portion of the professional development program. It's hard to imagine a professional learning community that would not welcome the opportunity to have their leaders not only actively participate in but also actually lead some of the professional development sessions. However, a faculty simply might not wish to listen to one of their own deliver the message or training—particularly if that training touches on difficult areas or professional practice that the faculty might have a tough time digesting. There will be occasions when data from the needs assessment points to severe deficiencies within the faculty. In these instances, placing the leader in the position of trainer can cause greater harm to his or her ability to connect with and lead the learning community, because he or she may be perceived as offering criticism or judgment, or even just as a know-it-all.

When professional development sessions are not provided by the principal or leaders in the school, the principal needs to weigh options, especially in the creation of a sound training budget, to ensure that these training experiences do not become lost. Sometimes, it is definitely worth tapping into an outside source of professional development to circumvent this difficulty and provide the staff a chance to participate with their principal as an active colleague in the training journey.

Examine the Role of the Literacy Coach

Many schools have adopted the use of literacy coaches as a way to improve the literacy practices in the school. Often, these coaches are reading specialists or Title I reading teachers who split their time between their primary job and literacy coaching. Some classroom teachers have also been used as literacy coaches. *Vogt and Shearer* (2007) have identified six distinctive models for coaching. Knowledge of these models can help a principal and coach determine which of these roles suits the school and staff the best.

Informal Coaching

The goal of informal coaching is to help individual teachers determine their own instructional goals and instructional strategies to meet those goals. There is little teacher observation, evaluation, or feedback. The emphasis is more on supporting the teacher outside the classroom to help them become effective, reflective thinkers and decision makers about their own teaching.

Formal Literacy Coaching

This particular model employs many of the features of informal coaching but adds a schoolwide dimension. Rather than focus just on individual teachers, formal literacy coaching involves more schoolwide staff development, modeling of effective instructional strategies, classroom observations, instructional feedback, and even coteaching. This is the most common model of literacy coaching.

Informal/Formal Coaching

Here the emphasis is still on supporting the individual teacher outside the classroom, but when asked, coaches make classroom observations and give feedback. Teachers still determine their instructional goals and coaches endeavor to help them achieve those goals, but this is done on a teacher-by-teacher basis and not as a schoolwide effort.

Peer Coaching

This is probably the most flexible model of literacy coaching, as it requires the coach to be able to take on a variety of roles with a teacher: planner, observer, modeler, and coteacher. The goal is still to help teachers become reflective decision makers and learn to evaluate their own teaching, but the coaches have more tools to use in helping them achieve these two goals. As a peer coach, the literacy coach has to be extremely sensitive in approaching any areas that may need to be strengthened.

Cognitive Coaching

This coaching model is built on a foundation of clinical supervision, but with a difference: cognitive coaching focuses on the teacher's inner thought processes so that perceptions and decisions are enhanced. The goals are to create a mutual trust relationship with teachers, promote learning by teachers and students, and help teachers realize that their students and fellow teachers are dependent upon each other to improve student performance. Three essential components of cognitive coaching include (1) planning conferences (goals and strategies), (2) classroom observations (predetermined in the panning conference), and (3) reflection conferences (teachers' perceptions of their instruction). These phases of cognitive coaching are designed to help teachers think about their instruction, whether it achieved the desired results, and what they plan for future instruction.

Clinical Supervision

Probably the oldest coaching model used in education, clinical supervision has been more widely used in the past in the supervision of preservice teachers by clinical faculty and university student teacher supervisors. It also has been a model used by principals and supervisors when evaluating classroom teachers. Once again, this coaching model helps teachers reflect on their instructional goals, instructional strategies, and their outcomes to promote the literacy success of their students. Like cognitive coaching, clinical supervision includes preinstruction conferences, instruction, analysis of instructional outcomes, and postinstruction conferences to analyze the outcomes and determine future instruction.

Principals may find that one of these coaching models is appropriate for the needs of their teachers and students. It is also possible that a combination of two or more of the models better suits the instructional challenges faced by their teachers and students. Regardless of which literacy coaching model is used, it should be accepted by teachers, principals, and literacy coaches if the model is to succeed.

Resource Coordination

The coordination of resources, such as volunteers, mentors, and tutors, can provide some out-of-the-box approaches to ensure there is time for training. These approaches vary and can include district support for more flexibility, community volunteer involvement, or release time supported by grant funds. If professional development programs generally lack effectiveness due to the lack of continuity and follow-up, then structures to provide focus, intensity, and continuity during each day and week will be a vital feature of success (Corcoran, 1995).

Examine the Role of Volunteers

Volunteers are vital to the success of a training program. Many times, volunteers are put into place in a building to read with students or to assist teachers in the classroom during guided reading time. However, volunteers are a part of the larger literacy program and deserve to be included in the training. This will provide consistency and an ability to work with the teachers. While volunteers should not provide direct instruction to our students in reading, they are a strong addition to the literacy program and must have some cursory training in order to work with our program and not against it.

Volunteer training programs can be held in the evening with dinner and should provide training in terms that the layman can understand. During the day, including volunteers in grade-level or department team planning can be beneficial. Parent–teacher organizations (PTOs) can be instrumental in recruiting volunteers.

Finally, Title I programs also require parent involvement facilitators or coordinators on the school to contact, invite, and coordinate volunteers. Allowing the parent facilitator to bring in community members and coordinate volunteer training will be vital to the success of the program.

Don't Forget Parents

PTOs or parent coordinators can also monitor the volunteers and the hours that they contribute to the instructional program. Simply having volunteers in the building to read to or with students each week is a good start, but it is not good enough. Linking them to the professional development program and making them part of the training experiences offered to teachers needs to be strongly considered in your overall vision.

The principal will be only one of a number of key players in the learning community that helping to build and accommodate the program of staff development. In addition, the principal will be a key leader in helping to continuously monitor the program through the collection, review, discussion, and sharing of data to mark student progress and achievement. As the learning leader, the principal can offer to cover classes with substitute teachers or even offer to teach a class or two while teachers meet for common professional training. This will allow the principal to gain hands-on experience in the daily workings of the literacy program and see firsthand the results and changes that the professional development training brings to the level of instruction and student achievement.

Plan to Assess and Monitor the Professional Development Program

Developing the means and instruments for assessing a professional development program is a tenet of the National Staff Development Council (1995), which recommends that "evaluation must be seen as an ongoing process that is initiated in the earliest stages of the program and continued beyond program completion" (p. 7). What gets monitored definitely gets accomplished. The development of various assessments should be tackled at the beginning of the planning process in an effort to identify and isolate those objectives that will be important to the teachers. This will ensure the integrity of the program, as the evaluations of the program will be guided by the reasons why the program of professional development was developed in the first place.

Both formative and summative assessments should be developed to gather data in an ongoing and incremental fashion. The formative data will allow the staff development program to be modified for improvement as it unfolds. The summative data will provide a chance for the participants to exhibit their broad understanding of the concepts and ideas presented in the program.

It must be understood that while the summative evaluation represents a culmination of sorts, the evaluations that are developed will need to continue to be administered long after the learning has taken place. Interviews, questionnaires, observational data, team meeting minutes and data review, and budget and material review are just some of the evaluation pieces that can be vital to the determination of the effectiveness of the developed program (Cook & Fine, 1997b).

An example of a formative assessment for guided reading appears in Figure 3.2. This assessment concentrates on three areas of guided reading structure that were consistently identified as areas of need by a faculty at one school. Other areas could be focused on or added to the assessment as needs changed.

As assessment data continues to be collected, further programs and fine-tuning sessions can be offered. This follow-up training will assist teachers as they practice

Teacher ____

Grade Level: Kindergarten ____ First Grade ____ Second Grade ____ Third Grade

Assessment: General ____________ or One Lesson (length of time) __

Directions: Check all of the characteristic descriptors within each category that best describes your teaching at this time.

Materials: My goal is to have all necessary materials present, organized, and accessible for use during the lesson, including leveled books in multiple copies.

___ I have a dedicated area in my classroom for guided reading. I am collecting my books and just getting started.

___ I have enough books to practice guided reading, but I have not constructed a leveled set. I have a dedicated area with some materials—easel ,white board, paper, markers, etc.—available.

___ I have constructed a leveled set of books that I am piloting; I have all materials ready for use in my dedicated guided reading area.

___ I have supplemental materials to accompany my leveled book collections, but they are not yet organized in the guided reading area.

___ A leveled, well-organized and tested collection of books exists and is ready for use/ being used on a daily basis in my guided reading area.

Groupings: My goal is to form small groups of children who are similar in their development of strategies and in the level of text they can read and to regroup these children through ongoing assessment.

___ I am just beginning to group children and am not sure what measures to use.

___ I teach the whole group; I do not know how to use running records.

___ I have formed and met with some groups in guided reading and am beginning to observe them more closely. I know how to take running records but not how to use them for regrouping.

___ I have established several groups for reading. I take regular running records and try to interpret results. I have not yet worked through grouping and regrouping and need more work in analyzing running records.

___ My groups are formed on the basis of systematic observation using running records; groups are formed so that individuals can use strategies effectively and groups are reformed based on assessment.

Engagement: My goal is to engage children's attention through the lesson.

___ I am constantly interrupted because my internal management plan isn't working; during guided reading, children's attention is inconsistent.

___ I can work with a group with a few interruptions but I have difficulty engaging all of the children in the group and focusing their attention on the text.

___ In general, I can teach a group with very few interruptions; children in the group are attentive, but attention is uneven across the group and from day to day.

___ During guided reading, children's attention is engaged; almost all members of the group attend; there are almost no interruptions.

FIGURE 3.2. Self-assessment for guided reading. Adapted from Fountas and Pinnell (1996). Copyright 1996 by Heinemann. Adapted by permission.

and master new learning in their instruction. Of course, student achievement data will be the ultimate measure of how well these practices are being implemented in the classroom.

Student Achievement data from both standardized and teacher-prepared assessments will be major components that allow the leadership team to analyze how best to adjust teacher instruction and the literacy curriculum. Formative and summative assessments should be major topics of conversation in team meetings and teacher conferences as a way to focus on the data and ensure the development of engaging instructional experiences for the students (Schlechty, 2002).

SUMMARIZING THE KEY ELEMENTS

To summarize, the key elements that should be considered in every professional development program to support literacy include the following:

- Understand that everyone on the faculty will be at a different place in terms of their instructional knowledge in reading. Just as the students come to us at different levels, so, too, are teachers at different levels. Many layers of staff development will need to be considered.

- Consider the long term. A one-shot training program with an outside expert often does not offer the sustained training that staff members might require. Sustainability and capacity will be key to any program.

- There will never be enough time to do everything that must be accomplished. Know the staff's limits and what they hold sacred. Do not tie up their valuable planning time with professional development, unless they ask for it or it becomes a necessary part of their planning process. Ask them what would work and provide time options. Don't rule out dinner meetings with child care provided, weekend seminars, day-long releases for training and discussion, before- or after-school learning programs, or off-site training for groups for better concentration away from the distractions and bustle of the school day.

- Budget is not a limiting factor! There is money out there that can be spent in creative ways. Many times, there are a variety of ways that funding can be spent, even though the money might appear to come with many strings attached. Consult with the Title I leader in the district and project a budget (think 5–10 years). When using grant money, have a plan for continuing the project once the grant ends, as grants eventually do. Talk to district administrators about the schools' vision of professional development—they should be a part of this planning from the outset.

- Do not be afraid to take risks with your money. Nothing ventured is nothing gained—you might be surprised by the results that you see with a program over the short and long term. If there has been sufficient research done and if staff members have been involved and are excited for such a program, then present those ideas. It will let the faculty know that you have confidence in them as professionals to carry the proposal, and it will usually produce some profound and powerful results that just might be the solution that you were looking for all along.

➢ Use internal experts. There are those in the building who can be tapped for their knowledge. As administrators, it is important to know the strengths within the school culture and who the informal and formal leaders are. Many of our classrooms have teachers who are those unwrapped presents and who, with a little encouragement, will be happy to support their colleagues by sharing their expertise and approaches with everyone. And it does not necessarily have to be at a featured program. Many times, a short share session with follow-up discussion at a faculty meeting on a Monday afternoon can serve the same purpose as a 2-hour program on the same topic.

➢ Be prepared to make adjustments along the way. Not everything in the process will go according to plan; fine-tuning will need to take place. Once your program is in place, it will need continuous monitoring.

➢ That said, the old saying, "What gets monitored, gets done" rings true. Build capacity through your evaluation and assessment programs to keep the expectation that continuous improvement is the norm rather than the exception, in your building. Administrative and peer observations should focus in large part on how well training is being used in classrooms. Monitoring and discussing the data—from running records to Diagnostic Reading Assessment to PALS to cloze passages and everything else that the district uses for collection—will need to become a focal point of planning meetings with teacher teams, if it is not already.

➢ Celebrate successes and each another. It will all pay off if properly established and executed. Even the smallest success should be noted and celebrated with colleagues. This is a journey that the entire learning community must embark upon. Have community celebrations for students' reading progress, a cake at the faculty meeting to celebrate gains, and individual recognition, both publicly and privately, to let faculty, community, and district leaders know that they are valued.

ENSURE THAT PROFESSIONAL DEVELOPMENT IS ONGOING

Many professional development programs concentrate around the quick fix—a workshop style program in which teachers participate in large-group learning experiences. Such a workshop is often delivered by a single expert who is hired for the inservice day and who allows for some dialogue, shared wisdom, and "make-and-take" approaches before leaving the site. Often, little is followed-up or monitored from that point. Some ideas from the training might be used by a teacher who happened to internalize some of the knowledge that was shared. For the majority of the teachers, however, there is no expectation that the principal will monitor the program, no collegial exchange or discussion as to how these approaches could best be executed, nor is there an expectation that there will be any implementation on a wide scale. In many other instances, professional development programs are underfunded or shortchanged on time and resources because of the traditional view that professional development is an event, not a process (Cook & Fine, 1997a).

Just as is the case with any change process, the professional development program that is being developed to meet the literacy needs within the learning community must have depth and breadth and must be given adequate time throughout the entire school day and week to thrive (Learning First Alliance, 2000; Sparks, 2002). Fullan and Miles (1992) powerfully emphasize this point as they make the case that far more time is needed for professional development and cooperation among teachers than usually is now available. Unfortunately, most people believe that teachers are only working when they are with their students, which leaves little time left for teachers to learn and study how best to improve their practice (McDiarmid, 1995).

Stigler and Hiebert (1999) point out that the United States does not have a structured system for allowing teachers to learn about their teaching practices and for developing any type of professional knowledge. When compared with other countries, such as Japan, this was particularly apparent. For example, Stigler and Hiebert (1997) found that Japanese teachers work in collaborative teams to identify and isolate instructional problems, plan lessons together, have a member of the team teach the lesson, and then reconvene to debrief, evaluate, reflect upon, revise, and reteach the lesson based on this input.

All of this qualifies as powerful elements of staff development. If the research links improved student achievement to strong teacher practice and learning about their teaching practice, then it would make sense that this powerful element of professional development should be found within any learning community. Yet time and budgetary constraints, scheduling, and an atmosphere of isolation and individualism continue in our schools, creating barriers to success in professional development that must be tackled by principals. Unfortunately, this isolation in teaching leaves us with an approach to professional development that makes it an event—a one-shot inservice day that is disconnected with so much of the daily work of our teachers—and not an ongoing process.

Building capacity and sustainability in a professional development program to support literacy may bring wider cultural change in the learning community, ensuring that the professional development becomes indelible for the teaching staff. Change is never an easy process, but the teachers must realize that there are to be larger cultural changes brought to the learning community that will establish ongoing, measured, and continuous support for professional development in literacy. If steps are built in the planning stages, the elements of change that will be brought to the school will be known, embraced, and accepted by the stakeholders. If teachers understand that they are supported in this journey and see that there are structures in place that protect and encourage collaboration, reflection, and learning time with one another—and that their efforts are supported and understood not only by the principal, but by the entire learning community at large – powerful results will be seen.

Case Study 3. Building Continued Capacity through a Literacy Intervention Team

At one school, the most cherished conversations that the principal can recall came from her contact with a group that focused on literacy and learning. The Literacy Intervention Team (consisting of Title I reading specialists, reading specialists, administration, and teachers) met monthly and more frequently when required to review the literacy program, the professional development needs and programming, and student data that kept pouring in monthly from the classrooms. This group was always eager to meet and confer on their progress and often came to faculty meetings prepared with analysis and insight that could be discussed, questioned, and analyzed each month to celebrate their successes and consider their needs for further development.

As a result, faculty meetings at this building took on different meaning. Rather than the principal simply standing and delivering information, the meetings focused on the results brought out of the Literacy Intervention Team meetings and became times when colleagues could share and celebrate some of their successes by modeling and demonstrating reading instruction. These meetings offered incredible opportunities to learn, share, discuss, and plan together.

Every one of the school's faculty meetings carried staff development hours and recertification points due to the simple fact that they provided a forum for learning, professional development, and discussion that led to continued consensus building, further needs identification, and opportunities for working on the literacy program. In addition, these times together allowed the Literacy Team to gauge progress, take back their perceptions to their own monthly meetings, fine-tune the program, and address any new areas of need that came to light.

Provide Continued Support

Continuous, consistent professional development is the goal. The wonderful thing about developing such a program is that is should take on a life of its own as it provides a continuous well-spring of learning for the faculty. The structures will need to be ongoing, with the attitude that professional development in literacy is not an event, it is a process. Discussion and dialogue that focuses on practice, data, and observation through a powerful program of peer coaching and classroom visitation will provide the staff with the basis through which they can launch these conversations with one another.

In addition, having mentors and volunteers available for continued conversation and coordination of support services is vital to ensure that the instruction is being supplemented by all of the parties involved in the literacy process. As these conversations continue to take place, further needs will arise that will provide chances to tweak or fine-tune the program. The goal of a continuous program of professional development in literacy is to provide each teacher with a larger body of knowledge from which to draw in dealing with more complex, challenging, and changing individual student situations and needs.

No End in Sight

So how long should such a professional development program last? Put quite simply, it should never end! Your faculty and staff and their professional needs will always shift and change. As Figure 3.3 shows, proper consensus building, implementation, and assessment of the professional development program creates a con-

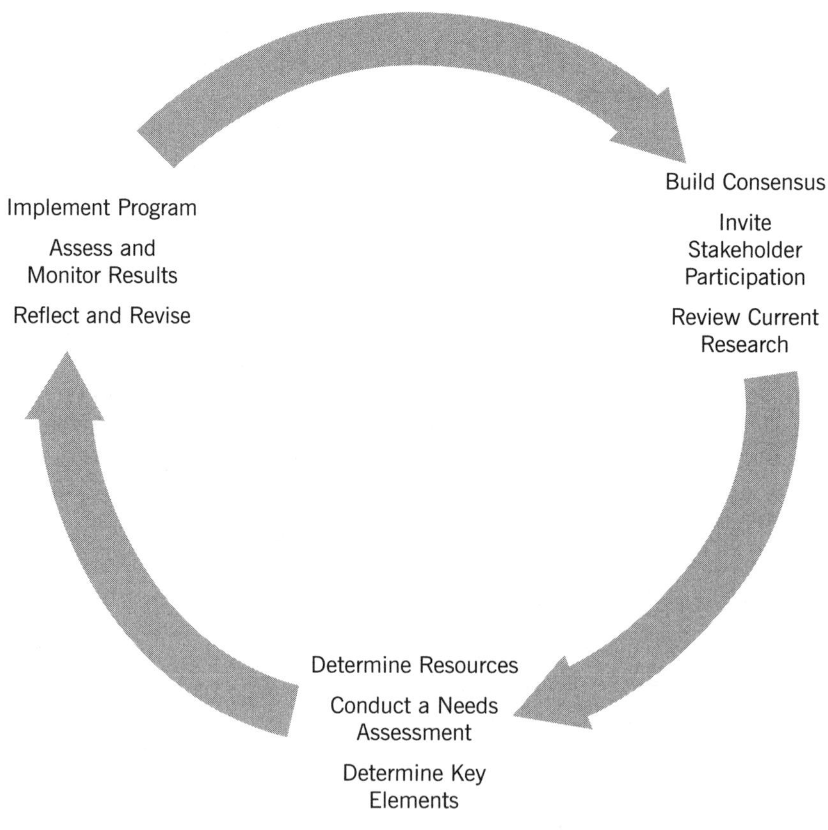

FIGURE 3.3. Building capacity for a sustained program of professional development in literacy—A cyclical model.

tinuous cycle of sustained, meaningful, and targeted teacher training that becomes the continued practice of the school. Furthermore, new faculty and staff members, parents, and community partners will always come and go, and their needs will change as surely as the positions and players do.

Each year, principals may hire many new teachers with a wide array of needs in reading. If there is a professional development plan in place, then it is easier to incorporate these teachers into the school culture. These new teachers can be given an overview of the system, a needs assessment in reading and literacy, and a menu of options, including courses, interactions, and book studies. The professional development system becomes the vehicle for conveying the school culture and the expectation that all members of the learning community will have the opportunity to participate in a professional development program.

The data that the professional development team cultivates and reviews will provide a window on how students are progressing in literacy as well as a window on what approaches and methodological approaches need to be addressed and supported. An effective and lasting system of professional development will identify those needs, address how best to meet them in the classroom, and provide faculty and support staff with the means to train, practice, and reflect on student needs.

Gaffney, Hasbol, and Corso (2005) show that professional development goals "cannot be maintained without the opportunity to take risks. Principals and teachers need to support one another as they learn collaboratively about what works in literacy instruction" (p. 14). The journey toward developing a system of professional development will not be an easy journey, but with strong vision, prior planning and assessment, programs that meet the individual needs of faculty and staff, ongoing and supported efforts for guided practice, reflection, and meaningful feedback during the instructional day; and sufficient time and resources, literacy professional development does not need to end. In this system, the principal, as an instructional leader, provides time and respect for staff members' efforts to improve literacy instruction. As a member of the team, the principal demonstrates a commitment to the improvement of instruction and student achievement.

Developing a sustained program of professional development in literacy will be a wise investment for your learning community. As principals, we cannot change where students come from, where teachers have been trained, or how community members choose to approach improving our schools, but we can create an ongoing and sustained system of professional development in literacy that involves the school community on a journey to meaningful student achievement. With such a system, principals and teachers will be focused on the school's vision and mission as they explore and practice what the research states is best literacy teaching practice. The entire school community will be united under a program that helps them know how to support one another and their children. Finally, and more important, students will grow to become strong readers, writers, and communicators, with an ability in literacy that will allow them to become productive and capable citizens.

CONCLUSIONS

This discussion of professional development has focused on the need for careful planning. After determining your human resources, several steps follow, including the need to review research, conduct a needs assessment, build consensus, and provide for individual differences within the staff development program. This chapter also discussed key elements of a program and ways to put the program together.

LOOKING AHEAD

The true success of any literacy program (and its accompanying professional development program) will be measured by how well students perform. Often, however, we as educators focus too frequently on the state and national testing mandates without relying on other valid measures of assessment. The next chapter will focus our attention on the variety of assessment measures available to classroom teachers, measures which can be used to supplement and enhance a state testing program. The use of a variety of measures will provide us with a fuller picture of our students' performance.

CHAPTER 4

ENCOURAGING AUTHENTIC ASSESSMENT

An education isn't how much you have committed to memory, or even how much you know. It's being able to differentiate between what you know and what you don't.

—ANATOLE FRANCE

With the high-stakes testing brought on by NCLB legislation (2001) and its impact on school accreditation through adequate yearly progress (AYP) reports, literacy assessment is especially important. In this age of accountability, state legislatures, and city, town, and county jurisdictions want to know how students are doing in their schools. Parents want to know how their children are doing compared to other students in their school and students at other schools and in other school districts. Teachers want to know how well their own students are doing in reading and writing compared to students in the same grade in other schools, and principals want to know how well their schools are doing compared to other schools. With this much emphasis on assessment, what can principals do to make sure that students are successful on national, state, and local assessments while also becoming successful readers and writers? To help better understand the role and value of literacy assessment in today's schools, we want to provide a context for seeing how the different levels of literacy assessment are related.

NATIONAL LITERACY STANDARDS AND ASSESSMENT

At the national level, three professional organizations have collaborated on national standards for literacy instruction and its assessment: the International Reading Association (IRA), the National Association for the Education of Young Children

(NAEYC), and the National Council of Teachers of English (NCTE). The IRA and NAEYC statement (1998) has a strong developmental emphasis because it focuses on preschool through third-grade literacy instruction. Within this developmental framework, both organizations also recognized the social, cultural, and linguistic influences on children's language and literacy development. A portion of the early reading and writing standards found in this joint statement includes this phase:

> ***Phase 3: Early reading and writing (goals for first grade)***
>
> **First-graders can**
>
> - read and retell familiar stories
> - orally read with reasonable fluency
> - use letter–sound associations, word parts, and context to identify new words
> - identify an increasing number of words by sight
> - write about topics that are personally meaningful (IRA/NAEYC, 1998, p. 687)

When the IRA collaborated with NCTE (1996), they created a set of standards to guide literacy instruction. The IRA/NCTE literacy standards go beyond the classroom by recognizing that students will need literacy skills to "respond to the needs and demands of society and the workplace; and for personal fulfillment" (IRA/NCTE, 1996, p. 21). Here are several standards that illustrate their real-world application.

> *Standard 1*
>
> Students read a wide range of print and nonprint texts to build an understanding of texts, of themselves, and of the cultures of the United States and the world; to acquire new information; to respond to the needs and demands of society and the workplace; and for personal fulfillment. Among these texts are fiction and nonfiction, classic and contemporary works. (IRA/NCTE, 1996, p. 19)
>
> *Standard 2*
>
> Students read a wide range of literature from many periods in many genres to build an understanding of the many dimensions (e.g., philosophical, ethical, aesthetic) of human experience. (IRA/NCTE, 1996, p. 21)
>
> *Standard 3*
>
> Students apply a wide range of strategies to comprehend, interpret, evaluate, and appreciate texts. They draw on their prior experience, their interactions with other readers and writers, their knowledge of word meaning and of other texts, their word identification strategies, and their understanding of textual features

(e.g., sound–letter correspondence, sentence structure, context, graphics). (IRA/NCTE, 1996, p. 22)

A closer look at both of these sets of literacy standards reveals overlap and general agreement on literacy standards to be used in our schools. For example, Standard 3 of the IRA/NCTE standards overlaps with the IRA/NAEYC Phase 3: Early Reading and Writing standard. In Standard 3 there is reference to understanding text structures like "sound–letter correspondence, sentence structure, context, graphics" which is similar to "[students] can use letter–sound associations, word parts, and context to identify words" in the Phase 3 standards. While Standard 3 is a general standard for all students, the Phase 3 standard is more specific to first-grade students. The complete IRA/NAEYC statement and standards can be found at *www.naeyc.org/about/positions/PSREAD0.asp*. The IRA/NCTE statement and standards is at *www.ncte.org/about/over/standards/110846.htm*.

National testing agencies have also become involved in national literacy standards and their assessment. For example, the National Assessment of Educational Progress (NAEP) is given in all the states in 4th, 8th, and 12th grades. In 2009, a new literacy framework will be used by NAEP for the first time, replacing the earlier 1992 framework. This new NAEP Reading Framework will include literary and informational texts as well as poetry. More informational texts will be included than in the past, recognizing the shifting nature of reading in our society. By the twelfth grade, informational text reading will comprise a majority of the reading on the test. The fourth-grade test will have equal passages of literary and informational texts, and by twelfth grade, the distribution will be 30% literary and 70% informational. The assessments will also include items that measure vocabulary knowledge as an aid to comprehension. When looking at the kinds of reading that will be assessed on the new NAEP, they are quite similar to the literacy standards seen in the IRA joint statements with NAEYC and NCTE:

Kinds of Reading to Be Assessed by NAEP

1. *Reading for literary experience.* Readers explore events, characters, themes, settings, plots, actions, and the language of literary works by reading novels, short stories, poems, plays, legends, biographies, myths, and folktales.
2. *Reading for information.* Readers gain information to understand the world by reading materials such as magazines, newspapers, textbooks, essays, and speeches.
3. *Reading to perform a task.* Readers apply what they learn from reading materials such as bus or train schedules, directions for repairs or games, classroom procedures, tax forms (grade 12), maps, and so on.

To see similarities between the NAEP reading standards and IRA/NCTE standards, look at IRA/NCTE Standard 1 and NAEP Standard 2. Both pertain to gaining knowledge about the world through reading a variety of different texts. For more about NAEP literacy assessment, read *The Nation's Report Card: 2005 Reading* along with more discussion of the reading standards that were assessed at *nces.ed.gov/nationsreportcard/reading*. Other national organizations, forums, and study groups have created national literacy standards that overlap with the literacy standards like the ones discussed above (National Reading Panel, 2002; Educational Testing Service, 2003). Keep these national literacy standards in mind as we turn to state literacy standards and their assessments.

STATE LITERACY STANDARDS AND ASSESSMENT

While the national literacy assessments looks at literacy performance by students across the country, state literacy assessment compares literacy performance of students across school districts within states. The state literacy standards generally reflect national literacy standards, although there is more specificity to state literacy standards and their assessment. The state standards also have more impact on a school district's literacy curriculum, instruction, and assessment because of their more detailed approach. They still echo the national standards, but speak more specifically about how teachers should instruct students regarding reading and writing in specific grades. We have summarized examples of two literacy standards from two different states (Virginia Board of Education 2003; California State Board of Education, 1998) to show how they reflect national literacy standards:

Virginia standards of learning for third-grade reading

Students read and comprehend fiction by:

1. Having a purpose for reading
2. Using prior knowledge in reading
3. Making predictions
4. Comparing and contrasting characters, setting, and events
5. Confirming predictions

Virginia standards of learning for third-grade writing

Students write stories and content-area reports by:

1. Planning their writing
2. Identifying their audience
3. Organizing their writing
4. Revising their writing

California reading standards for third grade

Students comprehend fiction by:

1. Connecting prior knowledge to their reading
2. Recalling key ideas in their reading
3. Making and revising predictions
4. Recognizing elements of characters, setting, and plot

California writing standards for third grade

Students write stories by:

1. Using a setting for the plot to take place
2. Including details and descriptions in their writing
3. Using awareness of their audience
4. Establishing a purpose for their writing

Note the similarities between the Virginia and California reading and writing standards. They each identify very similar reading and writing behaviors for their respective third-grade students. Notice also that these standards are more specific in identifying the reading and writing standards and what is needed to meet the standards than the national standards spelled out by IRA/NCTE, IRA/NAEYC, or NAEP.

Since state literacy standards and their assessment have a direct impact on the literacy assessment of students in local school districts, school districts use them when developing their own literacy curriculum and instructional strategies. School districts need to include them in their literacy standards or objectives to make sure that they are included in curriculum guides that shape the district's literacy instruction. NCLB and other national and state mandates also impact local school districts' literacy curriculum and assessment plans. The alignment of national, state, and school district literacy standards helps to ensure that teachers teach the literacy skills that will prepare students for the mandated literacy assessments that occur annually in school districts. How students in a school perform on a state's literacy assessments impacts their school's accreditation and AYP status.

LITERACY DEVELOPMENT BENCHMARKS

With so much attention is being paid to mandated national, state, and local school district literacy standards, we often forget about the developmental nature of learning to read and write. This is why knowing about the IRA/NAEYC standards is helpful. How can principals be sure that the literacy standards used in their schools reflect how children learn and develop literacy skills or that teachers are teaching them in a developmentally appropriate way? To help ensure that teachers are doing just that, principals need to be familiar with literacy development and the benchmarks that indicate that development. A complete list of developmental levels was presented in Chapter 1. In Table 4.1 we present a portion of those literacy development benchmarks to show that national, state, and local literacy standards can have a developmental aspect to them. When comparing the reading and writing development benchmarks, for example, with the IRA/NCTE standards or the Virginia and California literacy standards, there is a close match. The use of the complete literacy development benchmarks lets principals follow their state and school district language arts assessment standards while keeping a developmental perspective in mind as teachers assess and instruct their students.

LITERACY ASSESSMENT PRINCIPLES

Now that we have added a literacy development dimension to national, state, and local literacy standards, how should principals proceed with the assessment of these standards? Cooper (2003) identifies eight principles to guide teachers in carrying out literacy assessment in the classroom. We present them in Table 4.2 as assessment principles to consider for literacy assessment in any school. Schools can still meet national, state, and school literacy standards by using these literacy assessment principles with literacy developmental benchmarks as part of the schools' literacy assessment plan. This encourages principals and teachers to use student assessment as the primary guide for instruction in conjunction with literacy standards.

When reading through the assessment principles in Table 4.2, recognize the factors that can influence the results of literacy assessment, especially developmental, cultural, instructional, and learner factors. With these in mind, the literacy assessment carried out in schools will be more valid and reliable.

HOW TEACHERS CAN CARRY OUT LITERACY ASSESSMENT

We have looked at the connection between national, state, and local school district literacy standards and their assessment along with guiding principles for literacy assessment in the classroom. It is important for principals to be familiar with literacy assessments that measure the literacy performance of the students in their school. Literacy assessment can best inform teachers' literacy instruction if they consider a five-step literacy assessment cycle:

TABLE 4.1. Literacy Development Benchmarks

Beginning reading and writing (grades 1–2 or 3)

- Reading
  1. Sight vocabulary continues to grow
  2. Reading fluency grows
  3. Uses phonics and structural analysis for word recognition
  4. Uses context to learn words and their meanings
  5. Uses variety of comprehension strategies
  6. Has positive attitude about reading
  7. Begins to used text resources in all subjects
- Writing
  1. Demonstrates widespread writing
  2. Shares writing
  3. Writes in different genres for different purposes
  4. Uses the writing process
  5. Gains control over writing conventions
- Spelling
  1. Spells more words correctly
  2. Recognizes common spelling patterns
  3. Becomes aware of techniques to spell words besides letter-sounds

Almost fluent reading and writing (grades 2–4 or 5)

- Reading
  1. Uses all word recognition strategies
  2. Has instructional reading level at least at grade level
  3. Continues to increase use of comprehension strategies
  4. Enjoys reading independently in different genres for different purposes
  5. Silent reading grows
  6. Developing research skills through variety of media and texts
- Writing
  1. Writes for different purposes and audiences
  2. Uses different writing forms and genres
  3. Self-evaluates writing
  4. Shares writing
  5. Uses feedback in revision
  6. Grows in knowledge and use of writing conventions
  7. Makes links between reading and writing
- Spelling
  1. Grows in knowledge of spelling patterns
  2. Makes link between spelling, pronunciation, and structural elements in words
  3. Edits for spelling effectively
  4. Increases percentage of words spelled correctly in writing

Note. From Ogle and Beers (2009, adapted from Cooper & Kiger, 2005).

TABLE 4.2. Principles for Effective Literacy Assessment

1. Assessment is a continuous process that happens whenever a child speaks, listens, reads, writes, or views something.
2. Assessment is part of instruction. When students engage in instructional activities, their responses inform you.
3. Assessment is authentic. If you want to know how well a student writes paragraphs in an essay, have him or her write an essay.
4. Assessment is a collaborative, reflective process that allows students to learn on their own beyond the realm of the classroom. By making assessment collaborative, responsibility and respect characterize the relationship between teachers and students.
5. Assessment is multidimensional because multiple measures yield more reliable measures. Writing portfolios with drafts, self-assessments, revisions, and final products offer a more complete picture of a student's writing performance at the end of a semester of work than does a single writing assignment.
6. Assessment considers cultural, developmental, and learners' factors, and accommodations need to be made in all these areas when considering assessment measures.
7. Assessment identifies students' strengths as well as needs, and this provides a place to start and build upon as students move toward new learning.
8. Assessment reflects an understanding of how students learn to read, write, and use language.

Note. From Ogle and Beers (2009, adapted from Cooper, 2003). Copyright 2009 by Allyn & Bacon. Reprinted by permission.

- Step 1: Identify the literacy standard or objective from the literacy curriculum.
- Step 2: Develop and implement instruction to help students meet the literacy standard or objective.
- Step 3: Assess student learning based on the literacy instruction.
- Step 4: Evaluate student performance and the literacy instruction.
- Step 5: Identify new literacy objective(s) based on teacher evaluation.

The assessment cycle begins again when literacy objectives have been identified. The assessment cycle informs teachers about their students' progress in the literacy curriculum and provides useful information that can be shared with students, parents, teachers, and can be used to document student performance, the impact of the literacy curriculum, and instructional practices.

Authentic literacy assessment is the most valid and informative type of assessment to understand and to encourage teachers to use (Afflerbach, 2007). Authentic assessment looks at what students do in real reading and writing experiences and falls into two broadly defined assessment categories: formative assessment and summative assessment. *Formative assessment* is embedded in students' regular learning experiences and provides helpful feedback as they go through the learning experiences (O'Connor, 2002). For example, various steps in the writing process used by students as they work on a writing assignment can be assessed. Monitoring students' predictions as they proceed through a story is another example of formative assessment. *Summative assessment* looks more at the final result of a learning experience. The final draft of a writing assignment can be the object of summative assessment. Summative assessment takes place when end-of-unit tests are given upon the completion of a reading unit or segment of a writing curriculum. The assessment of student learning and teacher instruction should be important goals of each type of assessment. How students demonstrate their literacy learning can be helpful in pinpointing the kinds of literacy instruction students may need. The following sections describe various ways of doing both formative and summative of assessment.

Standardized Norm-Referenced Literacy Assessments

Standardized norm-referenced tests (SNRTs) compare the performance of students to the sample of students used to create the scoring norms. The tests are *standardized* because they follow identical, or standardized, directions for administering and scoring the results. They are *norm-referenced* because a student's test score can be compared with the scores of students in the sample used to create norms for the test. When arrayed, the sample scores resemble a normal distribution, or bell-shaped curve. Figure 4.1 shows what this bell-shaped curve looks like. The numbers at the base of the curve represent the percentage of scores distributed along the curve. When students take a standardized norm-referenced test, their scores can be compared to the sample norm scores and converted to standard scores, percentiles, or stanines. Standard scores use the standard deviation to determine how far above or below the mean score an individual score is. For example, if a standard deviation is 10 and the mean is 50, a standard score of 60 represents a score that is one standard deviation above the mean score.

A percentile score expresses in percentage form how well a student did with respect to other students. For example, an 85th percentile score indicates that the student did as well or better than 85% of all students in the test sample. Stanine scores also use standard deviations to express test scores and do so by dividing the normal distribution into nine equal parts. The fifth stanine represents the middle of the distribution, with four stanines falling below the middle and four falling above the middle of the distribution of scores. If a student has an eighth stanine score, the score would be more than one standard deviation above the mean of the scores.

A closer look at Figure 4.1 reveals how all the scores are related to one another on a normal distribution of scores (the bell-shaped curve). The numbers at the base of the curve represent the percentage of scores distributed along the curve. For example, 68 percent of the scores on a normal distribution of scores fall within (±) one standard deviation of the mean of all the scores. This statistical conversion

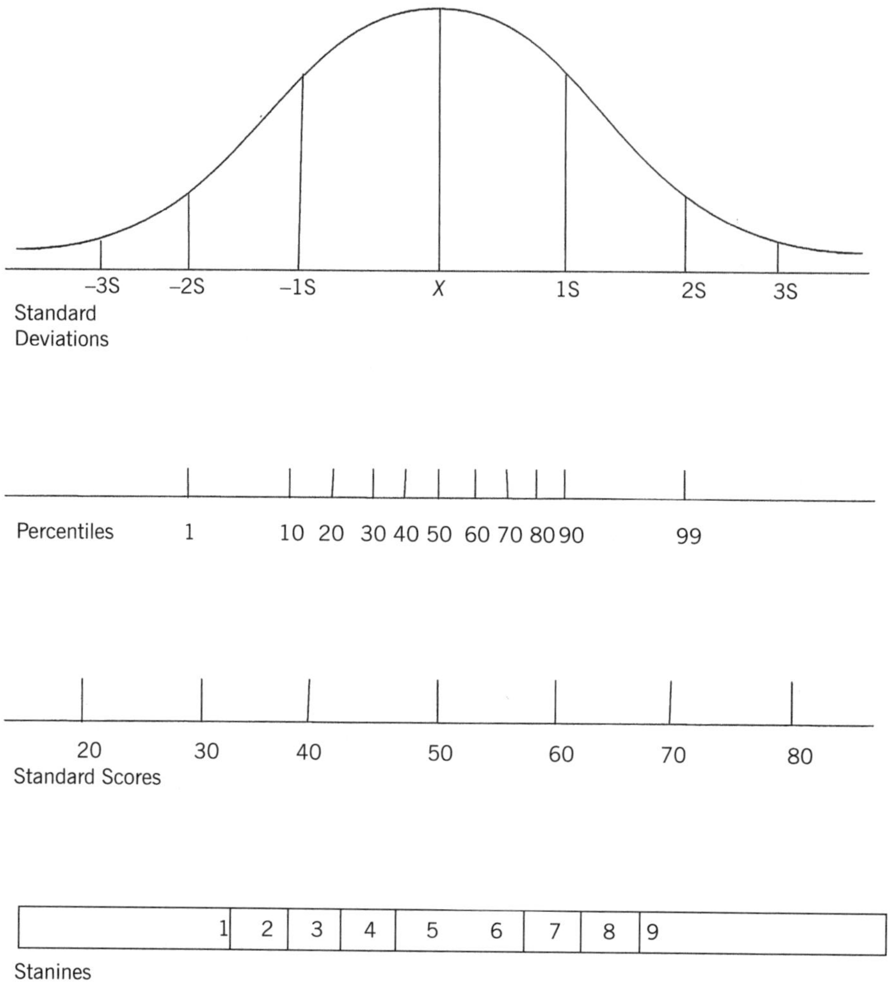

FIGURE 4.1. Standardized test scores.

permits comparisons across students, grade levels, the schools in a district, the districts across the state, and the state across the other states in the nation.

A school district may use SNRTs at the end of the school year to determine how students are progressing on general literacy measures like comprehension or vocabulary by using test items that reflect grade-level material similar to the material used in the different grades in a school. As such, these assessments generally do not yield helpful information about individual students on specific literacy skills because they are used for comparing groups of students. This can help to explain why students' performances on such a test do not compare well with other more authentic literacy measures like running records or read-and-retells. While the results of SNRTs may provide only a general measure of student performance, their ease of administration and scoring coupled with their general comparison value makes them popular assessments around the country. NCLB (2001) also requires the use of standardized tests for assessing the academic progress of students. Some of the tests that are widely used include Comprehensive Tests of Basic Skills, Iowa Tests of Basic Skills, Metropolitan Achievement Tests, and the Stanford Achievement Tests.

Standards-Based Criterion-Referenced Assessments

State-mandated literacy assessments often use standards-based criterion-reference tests (CRTs) to see if students have mastered the state's literacy standards. Let's take, for example, a third-grade reading standard: "The student will identify the author's purpose." A CRT item could have students read a passage and choose the answer that best completes the sentence that begins with "The author wrote this story in order to ____________." CRTs also establish the performance standard or criteria that students must achieve in order to "pass" the tests. Standards-based CRTs are important to know about because they impact the literacy curriculum that is developed in school districts and used in its schools. They have other significant effects on principals, teachers, students, and their parents. This type of assessment helps determine if a school maintains its accreditation, if students are making adequate yearly progress, and whether a particular instructional program can be used in the school. CRTs provide general information about the literacy performance of the students in a school, which teachers can use for grouping and instructional purposes. If the standards-based assessment is closely linked to the curriculum used in a school, it yields more specific information for instructional purposes. Most states have practice tests or previously administered standards-based CRTs online. Go to any state's department of education website to see what they look like.

Test Preparation Strategies

Test preparation is an important component of any school's literary assessment plan, especially in helping students get ready for state reading and writing tests. The Tennessee Department of Education provides an excellent list of test-taking strategies for students, teachers, and parents. For teachers, some useful strategies include the following:

1. Teachers inform students about the purposes for the tests.
2. Teachers have students practice different test formats that are used on the tests.
3. Teachers are familiar with the procedures for administering the tests.
4. Teachers know how to code student information correctly on test answer forms.

5. During the testing, teachers read directions carefully.
6. Teachers monitor to see that students mark answers in the correct part of the answer sheet.
7. Teachers follow carefully all test return instructions.

For students, helpful test-taking strategies include:

1. Students read and listen to testing-taking directions.
2. Students read, think about, and respond to only one question at a time.
3. Students make educated guesses when unsure of the correct answer to a question.
4. Students don't spend too long on a question.
5. Students skip really difficult questions and return to them, time permitting.
6. Students put their answers in the correct location on answer sheets.
7. Students completely erase an answer before selecting a different one.
8. Students check their answers after finishing a test, time permitting.

When, in addition to teaching and reviewing content to be covered on state literacy tests, teachers spend time developing test-taking strategies with their students and students follow these strategies, students are positioned to do their best on any test. For the complete list of test-preparation strategies for students, teachers, and parents, go to the Tennessee Department of Education's website at *state.tn.us/education/assessment* and click on the link to General Test Taking Strategies.

Observations and Anecdotal Records

Observing students' literacy behavior while they participate in literacy instruction or related activities is an effective way to assess literacy progress. Observations are useful for answering literacy questions such as: What steps in the writing process are students using? How do students discuss their writing in their writing groups? How accurately do students make predictions about their reading? To answer these and other literacy questions, encourage teachers to make observations of actual literacy events and activities and record those observations. The reading and writing objectives and instruction based on a school's literacy curriculum can serve as guides for what teachers should observe and take notes on.

Other kinds of classroom behaviors can also be the basis for teachers' observations (Acheson, 1997). These can include students' classroom behavior, their interaction with other students, and how well they complete assigned tasks. Teachers can use their observations to assess student learning as well as the effectiveness of

10/17/07

Donte' - needs ending for his report on reptiles

Megan - helps Donte' by telling him to go back to intro. paragraph and use those ideas to form ending paragraph. Like bookends.

Tyeshia - asks the group for help with her beginning paragraph

Teddy - offers suggestions for putting her sentences in a different order

James - needs help with sentence combining. Good topic for mini-lesson for him, Manuel, and Samantha.

FIGURE 4.2. Anecdotal records of a third-grade teacher.

their own instruction. Their observations can inform plans for future instruction. Figure 4.2 presents an example of a third-grade teacher's anecdotal records based on observations of students working in their writing group.

Checklists

Teachers can reduce the amount of time they spend taking notes while making observations by creating checklists of the literacy behaviors they look for in their students. Literacy behaviors can range from frequently observed to not seen at all. The checklist can also be a continuum of literacy behaviors that teachers would expect to see while students engage in a particular literacy event or experience. As with observation notes, when teachers use literacy checklists they acquire assessment information about student literacy skills as well as indirect feedback about their instruction. For example, if a teacher's instruction focused on helping students learn about sentence fragments, and sentence fragments continue to show up in students' writing, the teacher's checklist would signal the need for follow-up instruction in this area. Once again, literacy standards and literacy curriculum can give teachers guidance on what to include on their checklists. Figure 4.3 contains a portion of a checklist used for monitoring story retellings.

Story Elements	Student Responses	Points
Setting: (10)		
Introduction		
Place		
Characters: (10)		
Main Characters		
Other Characters		
Problems: (5)		
Identifies Problem		
Action: (10)		
Identifies Story Events		
Retells Story Events		
Outcome: (5)		
Identifies Problem Solution		
Describes Story Ending		
Total Points out of 50		
Additional Comments:		

FIGURE 4.3. Checklist for monitoring story retellings.

Interest, Attitude, and Motivation

The reading and writing interests student have, how they feel about their literacy learning, or what motivates them to read and write should also be part of the literacy assessment plan for a school. Assessing these areas shows students that teachers care about them and their interests and helps to ensure that students are positively engaged in their reading and writing. When a teacher can get some insight into a student's self-concept as a reader or writer, he or she can identify the kind of support the student needs. If students are reluctant to talk or participate in class discussions about their reading and writing, self-concept questionnaires can reveal factors that inhibit the students' participation. Interest inventories help teachers find out what students like to read or write about. This may lead to a re-examination of the books or reading material that are available to teachers to use with their students. Principals can play a major role in providing support for obtaining material that will engage students. Tapping into students' interests helps motivate them to want to read and write. Getting the best reading and writing material based on students interests is a primary responsibility for principals and teachers.

There are numerous assessment formats available for collecting information about students' interests, attitudes, and motivation. Teachers of younger students can have them answer questions or complete sentences orally. Teachers can have younger students draw or cut out pictures to depict their interests. For older students, teachers can have them write out their own responses. They also can draw as a means for expressing their interests and likes or dislikes about their literacy experiences. It is important that students feel trust for and from their teachers in order to give valid responses about their self-concept or interests. Make sure teachers explain that the purpose for gathering this personal information is to help them help their students learn in ways that are interesting and responsive to their concerns and needs. The Internet is filled with a variety of attitude and interest inventories designed for teachers to give to their students. Figure 4.4 contains an excerpt from an attitude and interest inventory.

Assessment Conferences

Assessment conferences are an ideal setting for teachers to talk with their students about literacy areas. They can discuss comprehension challenges and strategies to meet those challenges or they can focus on strategies for revising writing. Students can give their teachers feedback about what instruction is helpful or what additional help they need. Have teachers keep five things in mind when preparing for an assessment conference:

1. The conference should have a specific purpose.
2. The student needs to bring necessary materials or work.
3. The teacher should make notes of what is said by the teacher and the student.

After school I like to ____
____
____.

My favorite subject is ____
____
____.

My favorite TV show is ____
____
____.

My hardest subject in school is ______________________________________
____
____.

My favorite author is ____
____
____.

I like to talk about ____
____
____.

The hardest thing about writing is ____________________________________
____
____.

What I like least about school is ____________________________________
____
____.

What I like best about school is _____________________________________
____
____.

FIGURE 4.4. Excerpts from attitude and interest inventory.

4. The teacher and student agree on the follow-up to the conference.
5. The conference should be brief (not over 10 minutes).

The key to successful assessment conferences is the mutual respect and desire to improve that is shared by teachers and their students. Reflective teachers assess themselves as well as their students in these conferences. Figure 4.5 contains notes taken at an assessment conference with a third grader.

Portfolio Assessment

Some of the best sources of authentic formative and summative assessment information about students' literacy progress are student portfolios. Literacy portfolios can contain work in progress as well as completed reading and writing assignments. They can contain assessment checklists or rubrics used with reading or writing assignments. Teacher notes and student self-reflections also find their way into literacy portfolios. Portfolios encourage students to regularly reflect on their reading and writing experiences. Portfolios emphasize formative and ongoing literary assessment. They put greater importance on student-created writing products and reading responses in addition to the processes used to create them. They can also

Assessment Conference

Name: Tyrique

Date: February 12

Purpose: Writing

Comments: Tyrique is slow to start on his next writing assignment.
topic - whales - where to begin?
I want to see if he can brainstorm ideas about whales.
- He brainstormed questions about whales. This helped him to start.
-- Where do they live?
-- What do they eat?
-- How big are they?
-- Are there different kinds?
-- Do they have enemies?
-- How long do they live?
This helped. We'll meet again to see how these questions guided his writing.

FIGURE 4.5. Assessment conference notes.

promote greater interaction across all literacy areas: reading, writing, and visual literacy. To help teachers organize and manage portfolios, share these guidelines:

1. Determine portfolio organizational format with the student.
2. Decide on what kinds of reading and writing material need to be included in the portfolio.
3. Make sure there is a place in the portfolio for work in progress.
4. Make sure there is a separate place for completed work.
5. Include checklists, rubrics, and other assessment tools for use by the student.
6. Include student and teacher comments in the portfolio.
7. Decide how the portfolio is to be used in teacher–student conferences.
8. Establish rules for reviewing, adding, or removing material from the portfolio.
9. Use the portfolio for formative and summative assessments.
10. Create a schedule for using the portfolio with the student.

For literacy portfolios to be successful, they need to be used frequently so that they do not become just a repository for student work. They should be a source of pride about the process of learning as well as the products derived from that learning. Figure 4.6 shows a checklist that can be used by students to monitor their portfolios. For additional information about how teachers can use literacy portfolios, consult Peter Afflerbach's (2007) excellent chapter on portfolio assessment in his book *Understanding and Using Reading Assessment*.

Assessment Rubrics

A popular means of assessment today is the use of rubrics. *Rubrics* are a set of criteria used to assess student learning, and they lend themselves well to reading and writing assignments. A good rubric contains the elements to be assessed and a rating scale to determine how well the elements have been addressed. For example, a rubric used with a writing assignment might identify five elements that need to be addressed to successfully complete the assignment: content, organization, sentence structure, vocabulary, and mechanics. Each element on the rubric has a set of indicators that describe what should be found in the writing. The rating scale indicates how well the writer has included the indicators in each element.

Many assessment rubrics for reading and writing assignments, as well as formulas to help teachers create their own assessment rubrics, can be found on the Internet. Two excellent and free internet resources for literacy rubrics are *rubistar.4teachers.org* and *www.rubrics4teachers.com*. Teachers need to keep in mind that the best sources of information for creating rubrics are the reading and

Name: ________________________________ Date: ________________

Reading log: (What I read)	Writing log: (What I wrote)
1.	1.
2.	2.
3.	3.
Reading responses: (What I thought)	Drafts of my writing (First steps)
1.	1.
2.	2.
3.	3.
My favorite reading:	Finished writing:
1.	1.
2.	2.
3.	3.
In reading, I am improviing at:	My favorite writing:
1.	1.
2.	2.
3.	3.
In reading, I need help with:	In writing, I am improving at:
1.	1.
2.	2.
3.	3.
Reading topics: (What I like to read)	In writing, I need help in:
1.	1.
2.	2.
3.	3.
	Writing ideas: (What I like to write)
	1.
	2.
	3.

FIGURE 4.6. Portfolio summary sheet.

writing objectives and curriculum guides that they use every day. Since principals and teachers are held accountable for the literacy performance of the students in a school, why not use assessment rubrics that are linked with those literacy objectives? To help teachers create their own assessment rubrics, have them identify the objectives to be accomplished in the reading and/or writing task, the indicators of the objectives, and the scale that demonstrates how successfully the task is completed. For an example of an assessment rubric used with a persuasive writing assignment, see Figure 4.7.

Notice that the rubric identifies six elements that students need to include in their persuasive writing as well as a description of each rating of each element. The detailed statements found in the rubric help students recognize what they need to do to write a successful persuasive piece of writing.

Self-Reflections

Student self-reflection is one of the best ways to have students partner with teachers in the assessment of their reading and writing. Your teachers can model self-reflection by thinking out loud about their own reading and writing experiences or by sharing their own writing and self-reflections on their writing. In fact, you as a principal can do the same when you interact with your students. Here are self-reflection questions that your teachers can use with their students:

- How do I think I am doing in school?
- How am I doing as a reader and as a writer?
- What do I like about my reading and writing?
- What is hard for me in reading or writing?

Questions that stimulate self-reflection can be directed to specific reading and writing assignments or experiences:

- What was hard or easy about my last writing assignment?
- What kinds of words are hard for me to spell?
- Why would I like to write on this topic again?
- Why would I like to leave this topic behind?

Instead of questions, students can complete sentences about their reading or writing experiences:

- When I write, I need help with ______________________.
- Two things that I liked about this book are ______________________.
- Book talks make me nervous because ______________________.
- To help me in reading, I would like ______________________.

Ratings

Criteria	4	3	2	1	Points
Ideas and Content	Position is clearly stated and maintained	Position is stated but not maintained	Position is not clearly presented or maintained	Position or issue cannot be determine	
Voice	Voice is persuasive and consistently maintained	Voice is persuasive but not consistently maintained	Voice is not consistently persuasive or maintained	Voice is absent or ineffective	
Organization	Writing is clearly organized and clearly developed	Writing is organized but less clearly developed	Writing is less organized and clearly underdeveloped	Writing obviously lacks organization or clarity	
Sentence Structure	Sentence structure is correct and varied	Sentences are sometimes incorrect and are less varied	More sentences have errors and there is little sentence variety	Sentences are poorly structured and are not varied	
Writing Conventions	All conventions are correct	There are two errors in spelling, punctuation, and/or capitalization	There are more than two errors in writing conventions	There are many errors in writing conventions	
Word Choice	Vocabulary is varied to suit the position	There is some variety in vocabulary	There is little variety in vocabulary	Vocabulary is repetitive and has no variety	
Total Points					

FIGURE 4.7. Persuasive writing assignment rubric.

Regardless of the format, students' self-reflections can give principals and teachers insight into students' feelings about their reading and writing assignments and experiences. These insights, in turn, can direct future instruction.

Running Record Reading Assessment

In order for teachers to actively engage students in reading, they need to be able to determine the appropriate level of reading material for students. To help teachers determine the correct level of reading difficulty, they need to see if students can read accurately 90–95% of the words in the text. How can they do this? Teachers can obtain running records from listening to students read text out loud. To perform running records, they can have students read brief 100-word selections from books to see if they recognize 90–95% of the words. With a blank sheet of paper, a teacher makes a check mark for each word that a student correctly identifies as he or she reads the 100-word selection. Teachers can also make a running record by using a copy of the text that the child is reading. On the copy of the text, the teacher makes checks above correctly pronounced words. Whenever a student omits, mispronounces, or substitutes a word while reading, the teacher makes note of it on the blank sheet of paper or above the appropriate word in the text. Running records can be made in small groups or with individual students. They require a small amount of time but yield helpful information about the level of material that students can comfortably read (see Figure 4.8).

Running records can also reveal aspects of students' oral reading besides how accurately they identify words in the text. If students ignore punctuation while they read, this omission will show up on the running record. The nature of specific errors that students make as they read also is revealed with a running record. For example, a student may consistently omit ending in words. Another student may ignore the grammar of a sentence and substitute a verb form for a noun. Four questions that can help in analyzing oral reading errors are the following:

1. Are the errors frequent (more than 5% of the words)?
2. Do the errors change the meaning of the text?
3. Do the errors suggest problems in phonics?
4. What patterns emerge from the errors?

Answers to these questions can guide teachers in making instructional decisions about the word recognition strategies used by their students.

Students who do not recognize at least 90–95% of the words in a running text will be frustrated by the difficulty of the text, and the instruction using the text will be beneficial. Running records are particularly useful in preventing this scenario. As a principal trying to support successful student readers, it is essential that you make reading material available for all students at their instructional level, which is a 90–95% accuracy level. An example of a running record made on a copy of a text can be found in Figure 4.8.

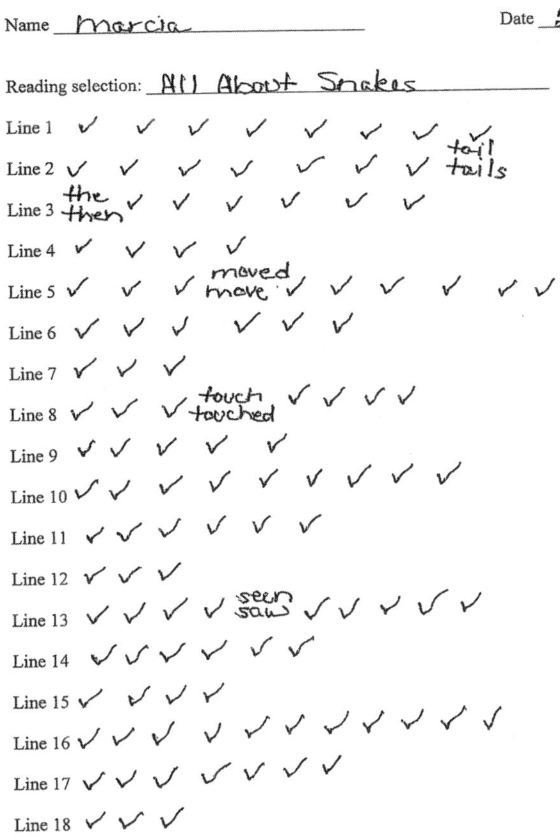

Name Marcia Date 2-15-07

Reading selection: All About Snakes

Line 1 ✓ ✓ ✓ ✓ ✓ ✓ ✓ ✓

Line 2 ✓ ✓ ✓ ✓ ✓ ✓ ✓ tail/tails

Line 3 the/then ✓ ✓ ✓ ✓ ✓ ✓

Line 4 ✓ ✓ ✓ ✓

Line 5 ✓ ✓ ✓ moved/move ✓ ✓ ✓ ✓ ✓ ✓

Line 6 ✓ ✓ ✓ ✓ ✓ ✓

Line 7 ✓ ✓ ✓

Line 8 ✓ ✓ ✓ touch/touched ✓ ✓ ✓ ✓

Line 9 ✓ ✓ ✓ ✓ ✓

Line 10 ✓ ✓ ✓ ✓ ✓ ✓ ✓ ✓ ✓

Line 11 ✓ ✓ ✓ ✓ ✓ ✓

Line 12 ✓ ✓ ✓

Line 13 ✓ ✓ ✓ ✓ seen/saw ✓ ✓ ✓ ✓ ✓

Line 14 ✓ ✓ ✓ ✓ ✓ ✓

Line 15 ✓ ✓ ✓ ✓

Line 16 ✓ ✓ ✓ ✓ ✓ ✓ ✓ ✓ ✓ ✓ ✓

Line 17 ✓ ✓ ✓ ✓ ✓ ✓ ✓

Line 18 ✓ ✓ ✓

FIGURE 4.8. Running record.

Informal Reading Inventory Assessment

Another reading assessment that helps identify students' instructional reading levels is the use of the informal reading inventory (IRI). An IRI is composed of word lists and reading passages that progress from lower to higher grade levels. Three reading levels that can be obtained through IRIs are the following:

1. Independent reading level (95–100% accuracy, 90% comprehension): Reads fluently and comprehends fully.
2. Instructional reading level (90–95 % accuracy; 75% comprehension): Reads pretty fluently and comprehends pretty well.
3. Frustration reading level (below 90% accuracy; 50% comprehension): Reads with difficulty and comprehends poorly.

By first administering the graded word lists teachers can find out how strong a student's sight vocabulary is and what word attack skills the student possesses.

For example, if a student scores at least 75% on the sight presentation of a sixth-grade word list, his or her sight vocabulary level would equal that grade level. Oral reading of passages indicates how accurately and fluently a student reads and how the student uses context to figure out words. Silent reading comprehension can be compared with the oral reading comprehension. IRIs are time consuming and must be administered individually to students but provide detailed information about students' reading behaviors while actually reading. This kind of information does not always surface through standardized norm-referenced or criterion-referenced tests if no oral reading is done. There are a number of published informal reading inventories (Johns, 2005; Woods & Moe, 2003; Silvaroli, 2009), and some commercial reading programs have IRIs that accompany their programs.

The scoring grid obtained from an informal reading inventory given to a fourth grade girl can be seen in Figure 4.9. The word recognition test reveals a sight vocabulary level of around fourth grade, an independent reading level of first grade, an instructional level of second grade, and a frustration level of third grade when considering the student's silent reading comprehension. What else can we see? She understands better when she reads orally than when she reads silently. If she is a fifth grader, this poses a problem given the amount of reading that she needs to do across her subject areas.

Read and Retell Reading Assessment

Teachers can also informally assess reading comprehension by doing read and retells with their students. To prepare for read-and-retells, the teacher selects a story for students to read that is on their instructional level. The teacher then creates a retelling outline that includes the following story elements: setting, characters, problem, plot, solution, ending. The teacher assigns points to each story element to establish a total retell score. Students are asked to read the story orally or silently, depending on the reading ability of the student, and then retell the story. When the student stops the retell, the teacher can prompt the student to talk about story elements that may have been omitted. The teacher should keep track of the elements given with and without prompts. The teacher can also check the student's understanding of story elements even before he or she is actually reading by having the student listen to a story that the teacher reads aloud. The teacher follows the same retell format used with students who read the story. Figure 4.10 provides an example of a read and retell done by a third-grade student. Notice that the student's retelling includes the names of the characters, setting, and major events depicted in the reading selection used for the retelling.

Writing Sample Assessment

The best way to assess student writing is to look at their writing instead of just writing test scores. This allows teachers to see how students are progressing and what areas of their writing warrants additional support and instruction. By obtain-

	Word Recognition (Isolation)		Word Recognition	Comprehension		
Grade	Timed	Untimed	In context	Oral	Silent	Listening
PP						
P						
1			99	90	90	
2	85	90	98	80	70	55
3	70	75	97	80	45	50
4	70	85	94	80	55	40
5	65	65	92	30	20	
6	50	50				
7						
8						
9						
10						
11						
12						

FIGURE 4.9. Informal reading inventory scoring grid.

A 8224 (grade 2)
Comprehension Questions

	No.	Score	Question	Retelling Notes
T	1.	+	What is this story about? (a boy at camp; Bill's walk in the woods)	boy who went to camp
F	2.	+	Did Bill enjoy going to camp? How do you know? (yes, the story said he was happy there)	yes it says he was happy
F	3.	+	Why did Bill go walking in the woods? (to look for leaves)	to see leaves and animals
F	4.	+	What kinds of leaves did Bill find in the woods? (maple and oak leaves)	oak + maple
F	5.	+	What else did Bill see besides the mouse? (a bird's nest; animal tracks)	a nest and tracks
F	6.	+	Where did the mouse go? (into a small hole by or in a tree)	into a hole in the tree
F	7.	−	What other animals did Bill see? (none; he didn't see any)	a bird
I	8.	+	Do you think Bill went on this walk by himself? What makes you think so? (any logical response)	yes no other person was in the story
E	9.	+	What other animals might Bill see if he goes for another walk? (any logical response)	squirrels and rabbits
V	10.	−	What are "tracks?" (footprints made in the dirt; something made by animals when they walk or run)	rows of dirt

FIGURE 4.10. Retelling notes on a second grader's read and retell. T = theme; F = fact; I = inference; E = evaluation; V = vocabulary. Based on a second-grade reading selection from Johns (2005).

ing student writing samples early in the year, teachers can get an overall impression of their students' writing abilities and instructional needs. These needs can include the use of writing process steps, content development and organization, sentence structure, and writing conventions. Since more writing yields more information, every effort should be made not to limit or restrict the writing but rather to encourage students to write freely and often. Once teachers have reviewed students' writing, they can better determine how best to teach them how to become better writers. Writing samples also help create instructional groups based on writing abilities and needs. This allows teachers to work with students in smaller groups on specific writing skills. After teachers gather writing samples from their students, they can assess how well students completed a writing assignment or assess more specific writing features such as how well the writing is organized.

Almost any writing that students produce can be used as writing samples. These include responses to student- or teacher-generated topics and student responses to reading, listening, or viewing experiences. Teachers just need to remember the purpose of the assignment and the evaluation criteria that was given to students before the writing commenced. These writing assignment parameters will help guide teachers in their assessment of the writing samples and in their planning of writing instruction.

Holistic Writing Assessment

Holistic writing assessment is summative assessment that takes an overall look at the final drafts of writing assignments. Holistic assessment examines final drafts to see how completely and successfully students have responded to a writing assignment. Its goal is to get a general impression from the writing and not to make an extensive analysis of every aspect of the writing. Holistic assessments are done quickly to see how a group of students or the entire class has responded to a writing assignment. Teachers can get the best results from holistic writing assessment by taking doing the following:

1. Begin by reviewing the assessment criteria that was assigned to the writing.
2. With these criteria in mind, read the final drafts quickly.
3. In one pile, put papers that successfully meet the requirements.
4. In a second pile, place papers that somewhat successfully meet the requirements.
5. In a third pile, put papers that less successfully meet the requirements.
6. In a fourth pile, put papers that clearly do not meet the requirements.

Teachers can assign four different grades that correspond to the four different levels of responses to the writing assignment. This can be a good opportunity for teachers to use the paper piles to identify students who may need additional help with the writing assignment or students who may need help with future writing assignments. It can also be an occasion for teachers to reexamine the nature of the writing assignment and its assessment criteria. Perhaps the assignment was ambiguous or allowed for more variety in responses than the teacher anticipated. It might even suggest changes in a future writing assignment that provide for more flexibility in how students can respond to the assignment. It is best to use holistic assessment to make statements about groups of students rather than individual students. Figure 4.11 shows an example of a holistic assessment rubric for an assignment in which students described their favorite subject in school.

Score of 4:	Papers select a single subject and describe it with concrete language. There are considerable details that are written in a well-organized manner. There are few spelling, mechanics, grammar, or usage errors in these papers.
Score of 3:	Papers usually focus on one subject and describe it clearly in less detail. Papers are less organized than level 4 papers. Spelling, grammar, usage, and mechanics errors areminor.
Score of 2:	Papers are less focused and less organized than level 4 and 3 papers. The papers resemble lists but are still describing something. There are more errors in spelling, grammar, and mechanics than in level 4 and 3 papers.
Score of 1:	Papers are brief and disorganized. The subject being described is not always clear. There are few details and many spelling, grammar, and mechanics errors.
Score of 0:	Papers do not respond to the writing topic at all.

FIGURE 4.11. Holistic assessment scoring rubric.

When looking at the assessment criteria in the holistic scoring rubric shown in Figure 4.11, we can see that they are quite general and designed to present an overview of how well the assignment was completed.

Analytic Writing Assessment

Another widely used summative writing assessment is analytic assessment. Analytic writing assessment analyzes the basic components in a piece of writing. Each element is assigned a weight that can vary from writing assignment to writing assignment depending upon the purpose for the writing. A popular type of analytic writing assessment is *six-traits writing assessment* (Culham, 2003). The six traits considered to be key elements to a good piece of writing are ideas and content, organization, voice, word choice, sentence fluency, and conventions. The first column in Figure 4.12 presents each trait with a brief description of the indicators of the trait. The second column shows the assessment rubric that the Jordan School District in Utah created to assess the six writing traits.

Six Writing Traits Found in Good Writing	Six-Trait Writing Rubric
1. IDEAS AND CONTENT • clarity and details • showing not telling • central theme	Ideas and Content __ 5 Sticks to main idea throughout, uses supporting details __ 4 __ 3 Occasionally wanders from main idea, lacks supporting details __ 2 __ 1 Has no main idea, does not support idea, limited information
2. ORGANIZATION • structure of the piece • strong lead • good ending • effective sequencing	Organization __ 5 Has clear beginning, focus, strong ending, and natural transitions __ 4 __ 3 Generally writes with a clear sequence, weak transitions __ 2 __ 1 Has no clear beginning and ending, sequence and details confused
3. VOICE • author's personality • audience awareness • changes voice for different types of writing	Voice __ 5 Strong individualistic style, sincere, suits author's purpose __ 4 __ 3 Style and enthusiasm inconsistent __ 2 __ 1 Flat, dull, lifeless
4. WORD CHOICE • clear and precise • words that reflect attitude and meaning • minimal repetition	Word Choice __ 5 Uses variety in words, fresh, original, fits author's purpose __ 4 __ 3 Uses general or ordinary words, only some variety __ 2 __ 1 No new or different words, weak, repetitive language
5. SENTENCE FLUENCY • sentences have power • sentences are a variety of lengths	Sentence Fluency __ 5 Paper is easy to read and understand, fluid and varied sentences __ 4 __ 3 Sentences are understandable but tend to be mechanical __ 2 __ 1 Sentence flaws make paper hard to read and understand
6. CONVENTIONS • spelling • punctuation • grammar • capitalization	Writing Conventions (punctuation, spelling, mechanics, etc.) __ 5 No glaring errors, easy to read and understand __ 4 __ 3 Noticeable errors that begin to impede readability __ 2 __ 1 Numerous errors, difficult to read

FIGURE 4.12. Six-trait writing rubric. From Ogle and Beers (2009). Copyright 2009 by Allyn & Bacon. Reprinted by permission.

If teachers teach their students about the six writing traits through instruction and writing assignments, an assessment rubric similar to the one use in the Jordan School District can be used to highlight and reinforce the qualities found in good writing. A great resource for information about six-traits writing can be obtained by going to the website of the Northwest Regional Educational Laboratory at *www.nwrel.org/assessment*. Information about the research behind six-traits writing, instructional strategies, and assessment for student writing can be obtained at this website.

Writing Assignment Assessment

Since good writing assignments are an important element in a classroom that supports student writers, principals can help their teachers assess the writing assignments that they create for their students by keeping some guidelines in mind. Murray (1968) and Mayher, Lester, and Pradl (1983) provide guidelines for good writing assignments. We have modified some of their guidelines and added others that teachers can use to assess their writing assignments. Poorly conceived or presented writing assignments can lead to student confusion and teacher frustration. This can be avoided with these writing assignment assessment guidelines in mind.

1. Writing assignments should encourage students to write because they care about the assignments.
2. Writing assignments should challenge students to gather, organize, and present information during the course of completing the assignment.
3. Students should be exposed to a variety of writing forms to help them decide which is best to convey their message to their readers.
4. Writing assignments should consider the experiential background and writing skills of students.
5. Writing assignments should follow the general structure of the writing process.
6. Writing assignments should help students learn something, solve a problem, or develop new insight about what their topic.
7. Writing assignments need to involve readers at various points in the assignment to provide helpful feedback and reaction to what is being written.
8. Writing assignments should make very clear to young writers what criteria is to be used when their writing assignment is to be assessed.
9. Writing assignments should be a mix of student- and teacher-generated topics, depending on the purpose of the writing.
10. Writing assignments should help students answer questions about their world and themselves.

Spelling Assessment

Spelling is another important area for literacy assessment. There are several ways that teachers can carry out spelling assessment in their classrooms. Teachers can begin spelling assessment in the beginning of the year by looking at the writing samples mentioned earlier. They can discover common spelling errors across students as well as individual spelling errors. They can analyze spelling errors to determine students' developmental spelling stages.

Spelling placement tests accompany most commercial spelling programs, which can also be used at the beginning of the school year. The spelling placement tests can help teachers determine their students' instructional spelling level. To determine the appropriate grade placement level, use the following criteria:

Score	Placement level	What to do
90–100%	Independent	Too easy. Go to higher level.
60–80%	Instructional	Place students in this grade-level book.
40–50%	Support	Place students but assign half the words.
0–35%	Frustration	Continue testing until you reach instructional or support level.

Another spelling placement test that can be used was developed at the McGuffey Reading Center at the University of Virginia. The McGuffey Qualitative Inventory of Word Knowledge (2004) contains words that are generally encountered at specific grades. Each list contains words with spelling features that can reveal the developmental spelling stages used by students. This spelling inventory is particularly helpful if a school does not use a commercial spelling program. An excellent resource, *Words Their Way: Word Study for Phonics, Vocabulary, and Spelling Instruction* (Bear et al., 2008), contains the McGuffey Qualitative Inventory of Word Knowledge, a description of developmental spelling stages, and helpful instructional strategies designed for each level of spelling development.

LITERACY ASSESSMENT AND DIVERSE LEARNERS

Literacy assessment may need to be adjusted in a school to accommodate the growing diversity of the student population. Diversity includes students from different socioeconomic, cultural, and linguistic backgrounds. It includes students with emotional, learning, physical, and social challenges. When teachers have students reading and writing at different levels, they also have diversity in their classroom. Principals can help teachers accommodate this diversity in the classroom while still carrying out authentic literacy assessment. For English language learners

(ELLs), consider assessment modifications offered by Lenski, Ehlers-Zavala, Daniel, and Sun-Irminger (2006) and encourage teachers to consider them as well:

- Use a multidimensional approach that includes alternative assessments (observations, conferences, portfolios, self assessments, etc.)
- Assess in nontraditional ways. Have students use visual rather than linguistic ways to demonstrate knowledge and understanding. Assess literacy learning in low-risk collaborative activities such as the language experience approach to assess oral reading fluency.
- Modify traditional assessments. Allow students to respond orally instead of in writing. Allow students to use their first language if a translator is available. Allow ELLs to use bilingual dictionaries.
- Allow students to collaborate on their own assessment. This permits code-switching. When possible, encourage parents who speak the student's native language and English to participate in the student's literacy assessment.
- Encourage self-assessment. Show students how to reflect on their own learning as a means of assessing their learning. Model this kind of assessment for students so that they understand what it is and how to do it.

As ELLs develop language and literacy competency in English, continue many of the same assessment techniques identified above, because they are the same ones recommended for all students.

IMPLEMENTING LITERACY ASSESSMENT

We have discussed national, state, and school literacy standards and developmental benchmarks to determine what literacy performance needs to be assessed. We have presented a variety of assessment techniques that range from norm-referenced tests to teacher observations in the classroom. Now we turn to the timing of literacy assessment in a school.

ASSESSMENT AT THE BEGINNING OF THE SCHOOL YEAR

Before school begins in the fall, teachers can begin literacy assessment by looking at students' progress reports and cumulative folders from the preceding school year. Learning about students' reading and writing performance during the past year gives teachers some insights into the instructional needs of their incoming students. Results of state-mandated reading and writing assessments (standardized norm-referenced and/or criterion-referenced) are usually available before school begins so that teachers can review them. As any principal knows, three months have passed since teacher comments were made or tests taken. Students can change over the summer, so this information is not always entirely reliable—especially if it is used to place students in reading programs.

Teachers need to begin collecting new assessment information about their students' reading, writing, and spelling abilities at the beginning of the school year. For example, kindergarten, first- or second-grade teachers might assess concepts of print, word, and story understanding. They need to find out which students are prereaders, emerging readers, and readers. They need to observe and note how students use the writing process. Second- to fifth-grade teachers might take running records of students reading out loud to determine independent and instructional levels of reading material for students. As mentioned earlier, running records can be used to find out which students are fluent readers and which students need additional support to become fluent readers. Teachers can get their students do read-and-retells or can administer parts of an informal inventory to determine how accurately students read and comprehend what they read. They can use graded word lists from the same informal reading inventories to determine if students need help with sight vocabulary development or word recognition skills.

With this beginning-of-the-year information, teachers should be encouraged to create flexible reading and writing groups and decide on the literacy instruction that will move each student forward in the new school year.

ASSESSMENT DURING THE SCHOOL YEAR

Literacy assessment should continue throughout the year once the initial assessment has been completed. With an eye on state and school district standards of learning, teachers need to monitor the progress of their students in reading and writing. This continuous assessment is important because it helps teachers decide who gets what literacy instruction and when they get it. Teachers can often use periodic tests or end-of-unit tests to see if their students have mastered concepts and material covered during reading and writing instruction. We have already discussed observations, anecdotal records of student responses to instruction, checklists, conferences, and portfolios. All of these are assessment techniques that can help teachers monitor the continuous literacy progress of their students. It is also helpful if teachers revisit literacy assessments from the beginning of the year to see if students have acquired knowledge or skills such as concepts of print, reading fluency, and story elements. Writing assignments and reading experiences can be assessed with rubrics that indicate how successfully students respond to both. Students' periodic self-reflections about their own work and progress can also be included in periodic literacy assessment. Regular review and interaction with students about ongoing and finished products in their language arts portfolios provide additional assessment information during the year.

ASSESSMENT AT THE END OF THE SCHOOL YEAR

As the school year comes to an end, many states assess their reading and writing standards of learning through standardized criterion-referenced or norm-referenced tests. These require considerable review time and considerable time to administer in the classroom. Even so, don't forget the importance of teachers gathering assessment information used for continuous monitoring of student progress in reading and writing. These include final conferences, writing and reading samples, running records, read-and-retells, checklists, and self-reflections. If teachers have used literacy portfolios with their students during the year, the end of the year is the best time to review these portfolios. Final portfolios should contain students' reflections on their work over the course of the year and final comments by their teachers. In many school districts, portfolios are a permanent authentic assessment record of a student's progress in reading and writing, which can be helpful to the student's teachers next year.

Monitoring Student Progress

Many school districts have turned to student progress monitoring to identify and keep track of students' literacy progress. Progress monitoring closely links student assessment to teacher instruction to determine if the instruction leads to student progress. After initial assessments are made in the fall, the periodic monitoring of student performance occurs. The progress monitoring, in turn, helps teachers decide on and adjust appropriate instruction that supports their students' progress. This continuous progress monitoring leads to the following:

- Better organized documentation of student performance
- More reliable accountability measures, especially important in high-risk schools
- More frequent assessment and instruction review that leads to better instruction
- Better instructional decisions that lead to accelerated student learning
- More effective means of communicating student progress to students, parents, and teachers

The keys to the success of student progress monitoring are the accuracy and frequency of assessment coupled with the instructional decisions based on the assessment, the ease of accessing the assessment information, the appropriateness of instructional decisions, and the effective implementation of the instruction.

Some or all of the literacy assessment techniques presented earlier in this chapter can be used in a progress monitoring system. School districts may already have this monitoring system in place, and they may be using it to assess the literacy progress of the students in their schools. If not, there are several websites where information about progress monitoring systems can be obtained. The National Center on Student Progress Monitoring is an excellent resource available at *www.studentprogress.org*. This site also provides information about response to intervention (RTI) which is closely linked to student progress monitoring. Students make literacy progress when teachers use effective instructional strategies as a result of the monitoring of their students' literacy assessment. When students' literacy performance improves, they have received an effective instructional response to intervention from the teacher. When it does not improve, student progress monitoring will show this and provide information for a more effective instructional response to students' literacy performance. Another source of information about student progress monitoring is the Research Institute on Student Progress Monitoring, which can be accessed at *www.progressmonitoring.net*. Here principals will find a description of curriculum-based management (CBM) used extensively in the progress monitoring models presented.

Literacy Coaches

To ensure that teachers make instructional decisions and deliver effective literacy instruction based on those decisions, more and more schools are employing literacy coaches. The two primary roles of literacy coaches are to assist teachers in their teaching and to support their teaching with professional development (Vogt & Shearer, 2007). The six models of literacy coaching identified by Vogt and Shearer (2007) were presented earlier in Chapter 3. Principals can select the literacy coach model that best fits the needs of their teachers and students, in doing so, and strengthen the connection between the assessment of their students' literacy performance and the instructional practices needed to improve that literacy performance. This is especially critical with schools that have been identified as "at risk" or "needs improvement" according to NCLB criteria.

CONCLUSIONS

This chapter addressed important factors for principals to consider when faced with the challenges of schoolwide literacy assessment: The importance of literacy assessment and the impact of national, state, and local school district literacy standards on literacy assessment and instruction; literacy development benchmarks; literacy assessment principles and the literacy assessment cycle; a variety of formal and informal assessment techniques for reading, writing, and spelling; assessment guidelines to accommodate ELLs; and when to implement literacy assessment in a school.

LOOKING AHEAD

Up to this point we have discussed literacy in the context of the school environment. In our next chapter, we discuss the importance of reaching out to families as we develop literacy programs. Some existing partnership programs are presented as are some ideas for conducting sessions with parents. Also included in the next chapter are some suggestions for working with parents of ELLs.

CHAPTER 5

REACHING OUT TO FAMILIES

Children are made readers on the laps of their parents.
—EMILIE BUCHWALD

Literacy must always be on the radar of teachers and administrators. One of the mistakes that can occur is the attempt to develop literacy programs and strategies in a vacuum apart from the world outside the school. A quality literacy program cannot be accomplished by teachers and administrators alone; it requires involvement and understanding from the home and the community. Schools that have charted high student growth and success in the area of literacy are those that have developed strong partnerships with the students' homes and the community at large.

When developing a literacy partnership with students' homes, the community, and the school, there are steps to consider that will facilitate the process. Let us first consider the "partnership" itself. As educators, we can become so focused on implementing a plan or initiating a new program that we overlook critical steps and areas of consideration that are essential to establishing solid home–school and school–community partnerships. The word *partnership* indicates a sharing of information, resources, and skills. Parents and community members must believe that they are equal partners in the effort to bolster student achievement.

The International Reading Association (2002) has stated that "educators need to view partnerships with families as an integral part of good teaching and student success" (p. 6). Family involvement is an essential component of effective literacy instruction. Figure 5.1 outlines the recommendations that the International Reading Association suggested as part of their position statement.

Be aware of	Be able to	Be willing to
the importance of family–school connections and be committed to the concept of partnerships with the families of *all* children.	build on family diversity in the classroom, at the school site, and in the home.	understand the goals and benefits of different types of family involvement, as well as barriers to their implementation.
the way cultural assumptions and life experiences influence interpretations of events.	work collaboratively with school personnel, other professionals, and with families and students to develop a common vision of partnership.	assume responsibility for initiating, supporting, rewarding, and monitoring various types of partnership activities.

FIGURE 5.1. Recommendations from a position paper on family–school partnerships. From International Reading Association (2002). Copyright 2002 by the International Reading Association. Reprinted by permission.

In keeping with IRA's recommendations, there are some points principals should consider as they set out to establish partnerships. The list is not exhaustive, but is designed to stir thought about the school's individual culture.

- How do we define "parental involvement"?
- Who is in our "community" (e.g., businesses, church groups, civic organizations)?
- How can we develop a cohesive plan that evolves from year to year and is sustainable?
- How will we incorporate strategies that are child-specific?
- What considerations and limitations do our families have?
- How will we recognize our families' individual needs?
- What is the purpose of our program?
- How will we communicate with our families and community?
- Do we understand that trust is an essential factor?
- How will we evaluate the program?
- What steps will we take to reward the increased time commitment required by teachers and administrators?
- What are the budget implications?

THE RESEARCH

Before discussing the steps for implementing a successful literacy partnership program, we should briefly consider research that supports home–school and school–community partnerships. First, we must acknowledge that literacy begins at home. Studies have shown that the love for reading is often established at an early age by a child's first teacher(s), Mom and/or Dad (Robb, 2003; National Research Council, 1999). This is not to suggest that the love of literacy cannot be instilled once a child enters school. It is incumbent upon the school to inspire the desire to read in students. As schools set out on this journey, an invitation should be extended to parents to join them. Parents tend to respond positively when an invitation to participate is extended by their child's teacher (Reed, Jones, Walker, & Hoover-Dempsey, 2000). In addition, teacher attitude toward parent involvement can affect whether or not parents view their role in a partnership positively (Hoover-Dempsey & Sandler, 1997). Evidence also suggests that parental involvement in the education of children is critical to overall student achievement (IRA, 2002; Padak & Rasinski, 2003). This is especially true for children who come from low-income and culturally diverse families. *The Early Catastrophe: The 30 Million Word Gap by Age 3*, a study conducted by Hart and Risley (2003), is an important body of knowledge that points to the urgency of providing children of poverty with rich literacy and vocabulary acquisition as early as possible in their development. Hart and Risley conclude that the longer the effort to provide literacy intervention is delayed, the greater the challenge becomes to equalize the achievement. Partnerships between home and school facilitate and instill confidence in parents about the school their children attend (IRA, 2002). In particular, literacy partnership(s) foster positive attitudes in children and parents toward reading (Padak & Rasinski, 2003).

Joyce Epstein, director of the Center on School, Family, and Community Partnerships at Johns Hopkins University, suggests that school communities should organize partnership programs that provide various types of involvement. (DeLisio, 2009). She has identified five types of involvement that she believes schools can employ.

1. Communicating involves communicating regularly with families about student progress and school programs.
2. Volunteering includes trying to improve recruitment, training, jobs, and schedules of volunteers so that more families become involved.
3. Learning at home provides opportunities for families to engage in learning activities with their children at home,
4. Decision making includes families in school decision-making opportunities.
5. Collaborating with the community provides for coordination to provide services for families.

This approach is comprehensive because it recognizes the various roles that families can have as schools plan meaningful involvement for them.

As Epstein mentions, school–community partnerships are also important in the literacy program. Research indicates that both students and businesses gain from school–community partnerships. Partnering with businesses and the community increases students' awareness of the world outside of school, and, in many cases, outside their immediate community. Students gain something called "social capital," which is "their ability to move successfully in the larger world beyond their immediate neighborhoods and communities" (Berg, Melaville, & Blank, 2007). School–community collaboration is viewed as a way to provide additional support to schools, students, and parents (IRA, 2002). One study suggests that "weaving together" school and community resources will help students gain a better sense of the relationship between what they learn at school and the world of work (Berg et al., 2007).

A PRINCIPAL'S STORY

"Good, better, best. Never let it rest until your good is better and your better is your best!" This is the mantra of Mrs. Elizabeth Beckhouses's leadership. Liz, as she is affectionately known, has never been satisfied with arriving to work at 8:00 A.M. and leaving at 4:00 P.M., but rather she has always looked for innovative ways to keep families and her school community connected to learning. When you see Liz in action as the principal of her school, you quickly recognize a person whose style embraces enthusiasm and a zeal for student learning. Teachers, parents, and students alike embrace Liz's mission and dedication, which has created an exceptional environment for learning. What is unique about Liz is that while she possesses high expectations for each student, she has created opportunities to connect with families beyond the 3:20 P.M. bell, and more importantly, beyond the schoolhouse.

This kind of leadership became the impetus for a community partnership entitled "Luggage for Learning," which is discussed later in this chapter. During the time Liz served at another school, she and a group of committed teachers were determined to reach out to families in a way that would be fun but also educationally meaningful. They began to contact community leaders in an effort to generate interest in hosting a school literacy night once a week during which students and their families could participate in math and literacy activities. The program would seek to create a stronger bond for learning between children and their families while also fostering a stronger relationship between the school and families.

Their efforts generated the interest and opportunity that Liz wanted—a community-based building in which to house her outreach program and committed teachers who were willing to create literacy and math activity packets and make the sacrifice to show up on a consistent basis as facilitators. Liz noted that there are two important ingredients when building partnerships for learning with families: (1) a supportive staff and (2) the willingness of the community and parents to participate. A true testament of the success of this type of partnership is, as Liz stated, "to see the excitement for learning from both students and parents and to have students want to continue to participate in the program as they move to middle school." It is not surprising to us that Liz initiated a similar program when she became the principal at another school.

This is just one story that demonstrates the impact of reaching out to families (E. Beckhouse, personal communication, November 2007). While Liz sees the partnerships that were created as a natural sequence of events that resulted in stronger relationships with students and their families, it is this kind of vision and action that will give your school a stronger foundation for teaching and learning.

CIRCLES OF INFLUENCE

Parents, the community, and schools create *circles of influence* that are the foundation to the success of a literacy program. It is important to recognize that each segment of the partnership is essential to achieving the successful outcome desired (i.e., fluent readers). When these circles overlap, they create a stronger influence that propels student achievement. Definitive roles, however, must be established for each segment of the partnership. Figure 5.2 demonstrates how each circle adds

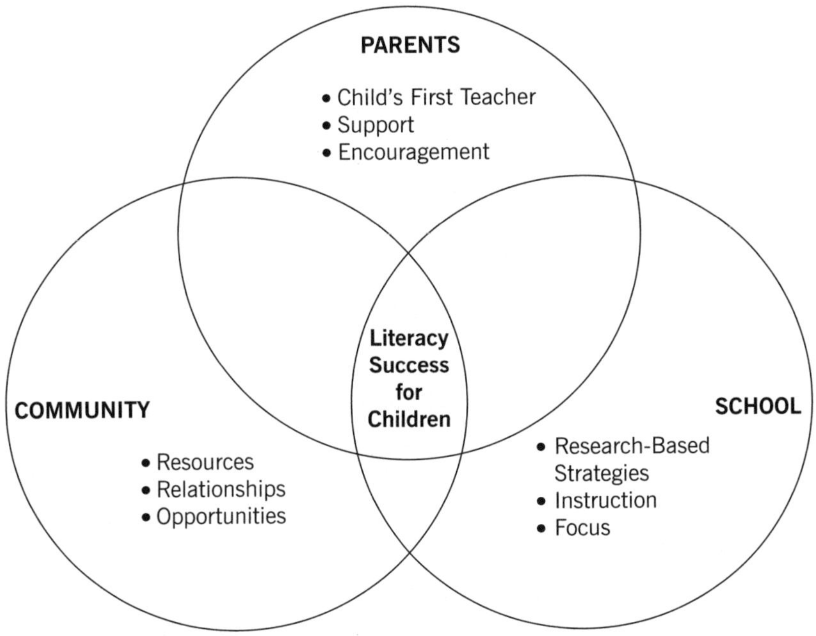

FIGURE 5.2. Circles of influence.

value to the partnership as it strives toward a common goal. This conceptual model requires that the principal be willing to share leadership with other stakeholders. Ogle (2007) suggests that building these partnerships is critical to building successful reading programs.

STEPS FOR IMPLEMENTING A SUCCESSFUL PARTNERSHIP

When preparing to implement a successful literacy program, principals should consider several steps. These steps are important planning elements to ensure that your program is successful.

1. Consider your stakeholders.
   - Who from the school and school district must and should be a part of the process and the program?
   - What students would benefit from the program?
   - Who in the community should be a part of the process and program?
2. Determine the level of responsibility for those involved.
   - What will the school provide?
   - What will parents bring to the table?
   - How can members of the community/businesses support the effort?
3. Identify the required human and financial resources.
   - What community group/organization/business might be willing to sponsor the program financially?
   - Are there civic groups that would be willing to partner with the school?
   - Is there a group of retirees that would be willing to lend their expertise to the program?

As we look at sample parent involvement programs, we will consider three elements: (1) school responsibilities, (2) parent involvement, and (3) community involvement. Prior to deciding on a program, action planning must take place.

Develop an Action Plan

As principal, your primary responsibility is to bring together a team of individuals who support the effort and vision of partnership outreach as it relates to literacy, who understand the importance of literacy, and who are committed to the partnership. The team should consist of several stakeholders: at least one building-level administrator (to help guide the process), a central office administrator (to provide district-level support), reading specialist(s), grade-level and/or subject-specific teachers, parents, and community members.

Together the team must devise an action plan. An action plan not only outlines the important steps that must be taken to implement a literacy partnership program, but, more important, identifies who will be responsible for various aspects of the program, outline how, and establish important deadlines for completion of the actions. Figure 5.3 is a sample action plan that can be adapted for your partnership efforts.

What	Who	How	When
Determine the goal(s) of the partnership(s)	Teachers/ administrators	• Solicit ideas from teachers	By 6/15/09
Assemble a team of stakeholders	Principal	• Personal contact with individuals	By 8/3/09
Coordinate initial meeting time and location	Principal	• Memos, letters, e-mails, phone calls	By 8/17/09
Meet and determine a timeline for implementation	Literacy team		By 9/4/09
Design/adapt literacy partnership program • Gather materials	Literacy team	• Develop draft • Review with stakeholders; revise • Finalize draft	By 9/10/09
Establish communication/ marketing plan	Literacy team	• (see *Communicate about the Partnership*, p. 137)	By 11/12/09
Implement literacy partnership program	Literacy team	• Provide parents and community with information and training sessions • Hold sessions bimonthly	By 1/15/10
Evaluate literacy partnership program	Literacy team	• Survey partnership participants (parents and community members) • Analyze student test scores/ grades/ fluency, etc.	Spring 2010
Make adjustments	Literacy team	• Use data from surveys and student achievement scores	Summer 2010

FIGURE 5.3. Sample action plan.

Examine Existing Literacy Partnership Programs

When establishing or refining your school's partnership program, a good starting point is to become aware of what is already available. Using existing frameworks or models will save you and members of your team time that can be directed toward implementation. Below are some literacy frameworks that can easily be adapted to meet any school's literacy partnership efforts.

Luggage for Learning

Luggage for Learning is an literacy-based outreach program designed to build interactions among teachers, parents, and children at a community-based center. Teachers develop grade-specific games that reinforce essential concepts and skills taught at school. The premise of Luggage for Learning is to provide enrichment and not remediation. A relationship is established with a community-based organization that will provide space where families and teachers can come together for the purpose of literacy enrichment.

It is important that the logistics, such as site, room location, time, and day, are worked out before getting started. Remember, we are creatures of habit and will soon lose interest if the program logistics are not consistently carried out. The sessions are led by teachers and are kept on an informal level. While teachers lead the activities, parents are able to observe and determine their level of participation.

Parents or guardians, however, must remain for the entire session. This helps to ensure some level of transfer at the child's home. In addition, children are allowed to take the literacy activity home and keep it for a 2-week period. Directions for techniques and strategies that can be used when engaging the child are also sent home with the activity. As a result, student learning is directly affected through practice in specific skills, and parents are shown ways to expand learning beyond homework. Such a program not only creates informal settings for parents and teachers to bond in developing mutually positive relationships but also enhances student learning.

Implementing Luggage for Learning

1. School responsibilities

   - Determine school contact person.
   - Identify cohort of interested teachers.
   - Develop activity packets.
   - Establish community partnerships.

- Set up time and day
- Communicate with parents and other community partners.

2. Parent responsibilities

   - Make a commitment to the partnership.
   - Ensure child is present for each session.
   - Remain on site and engaged during entire session.
   - Observe activities.

3. Community (business) responsibilities

   - Provide location for sessions.
   - Ensure location is available for each session.
   - Provide volunteers to participate in the program.

Partners in Print

Partners in Print is designed for parents and teachers to engage in literacy development. The program was originally designed for students in grades kindergarten through 2; however, it can be adapted for older children and their parents. In order for the program to be successful, the team should include teachers, administrators, reading specialists, volunteers, and, of course, parents.

Partners in Print is a program that is held at the school, where parents receive training (one night) at the beginning of the school year. The focus of the program is to teach parents basic literacy instruction. It is designed to expose parents to literacy strategies that can be used at home to support the literacy instruction that occurs in the classroom. Parents may be given free literacy resources such as books, magnetic letters, journal booklets for writing, markers, or a cassette player so students can record themselves for fluency purposes.

This program is held once a month, with dinner provided as well as child care for siblings. At some point during the session, the parent is partnered with his or her child so that the parent can practice the literacy strategies they have learned.

Implementing Partners in Print

1. School responsibilities

   - Provide location, materials, and training.
   - Assist parents with literacy strategies.
   - Provide child care for siblings.

2. Parent responsibilities

- Make a commitment to the partnership.
- Ensure child is present for each session.
- Remain on site and engaged during entire session.
- Observe and participate in activities.

3. Community (business) responsibilities

- Assist in providing child care.
- Provide refreshments/dinner.

(For additional information on *Partners in Print*, visit their website at *www.arac.umd/partners_print.html.*)

Early Years Literacy Program

The Early Years Literacy Program is designed for students in grades kindergarten through 3. Parent–school partnership is key in the implementation of this program, as its intended focus is to strengthen the overall home–school relationship. In four sessions, parents learn how children learn to speak, listen, read, and write; explore learning experiences in the home and in the school; determine how to make learning easier for their children; and establish ways to work with the school to support literacy.

The program is divided into three stages. Stage 1 addresses "Teaching Readers," Stage 2 addresses "Teaching Writers," and Stage 3 covers "Teaching Speakers and Listeners." The program guide contains a detailed outlined. It provides guidance on everything from talking points for the briefing session to the number of minutes required for each portion of each session. Sessions are held weekly, and session facilitators are provided with handouts and worksheets for parents. Parents and session facilitators (teachers and/or administrators) are asked to maintain a diary for notes, reflections, observations, and questions. The program encourages discussion groups to continue even after the official program has concluded.

Implementing the Early Years Literacy Program

1. School responsibilities

- Provide location, materials, and training.
- Assist parents with literacy strategies.
- Provide child care for siblings.
- Provide refreshments.

2. Parent responsibilities

    - Make a commitment to the partnership.
    - Remain on site and engaged during entire session.
    - Observe and participate in activities.
    - Maintain a diary.
    - Implement strategies at home.

3. Community (business) responsibilities

    - Assist in providing child care.
    - Provide volunteers for children whose parents cannot participate.

(For more information on the Early Years Literacy Program, see Hammond & Reynolds, 1999.)

Communicate about the Partnership

Once an action plan has been developed and a literacy program selected, steps must be taken to get the word out. Communication can and should occur through several channels. Listed below are a variety of avenues you may already have at your disposal.

- School/district newsletter
- Sending flyers home with students
- Automated calling system
- E-mail
- School/district website
- Student-created invitations
- Community–Parent coffee/tea (provide child care)
- Parent–teacher association meetings
- Literacy fun night
- Teacher-initiated invitations
- Ad in the local newspaper
- Contacting human resources offices of local businesses
- Personal visits to local businesses to tell them about the program
- Local cable channel advertisement

Sample Flyer

Sample Newspaper Ad

Promise Elementary School
Join us for
"Literacy Is Fun" Night

There will be *dinner, games, prizes, puppet shows*, and **BOOKS**!

Friday, October 24, 2009
7:00 p.m. – 9:00 p.m.
Call 803-555-1212
For more information

Student-created invitation

Mom & Dad,
Come to Fun Night at our school. There will be food, games, prizes, and books. Please come on October 24th at 7:00 p.m.
Johnny

FIGURE 5.4. Sample communication tools.

Figure 5.4 contains examples of some communication tools that have been used in schools. The best way to find samples is to consult with other schools in your area to see what they have done.

BRINGING EVERYONE TOGETHER

The First Meeting

The initial parent meeting for your literacy program should be inviting and fun. Parents should not be bogged down with a lot of jargon and/or materials; provide an overview of the literacy program and its purpose. Introduce the literacy team so that parents will know that decisions regarding the literacy program were not made in isolation but by a group of individuals representing all stakeholders, including parents. Make parents aware that this is a *partnership* and delineate the role of the partners. Answer the questions "What will the school provide?" and "What will be required of the parents?"

Because families are so busy these days, be sure to include the time element (i.e., how much time this "partnership" will require). Keep in mind the points to consider mentioned earlier in this chapter. Also, be sure to explain the benefits of the literacy program and how it is designed to help children in the areas of reading, comprehension, and fluency. Explain the importance of literacy as it relates to all other subjects: math, social studies, science, and so on. Inform parents about training that may be required and the training schedule.

Remember, most parents are not literacy experts or educators. The school must provide guidance and simple strategies that can be employed effectively at home.

Community Involvement

Partnerships between the school and the community are also important in fostering literacy. Most businesses participate in socially responsible behavior toward the community in which they exist. Schools should not hesitate to reach out to them. Why not tap into their sense of giving to the community by extending an invitation to partner with your school? After all, you coexist in the same local and share a body of individuals (parents who work for local businesses), services (public transportation, parks, etc.), and a common interest in the well-being and the success of the young people in the community. Help businesses understand that a partnership with the school is an investment in their future as well as the future of students. Today's students are tomorrow's employees.

A Spiral Framework

As stated earlier in the chapter, it is important to spend time establishing a strong literacy partnership that will enhance the school's literacy program. One way to ensure success is to implement a partnership program that has a spiral framework (see Figure 5.5). A spiral framework is one that will extend student learning each year based on your school's literacy program, helping to avoid fragmentation. Selecting activities that are conducive to enriching the program and strengthening the partnership(s) is imperative for solidification. Knowing what activities to look for and incorporate into the program will help in this process. This can be easily accomplished by making certain that literacy activities and focus are grade-level specific and build from year to year. This is a helpful tool to avoid designing a remediation program rather than an enrichment literacy partnership program.

Sample Literacy Activities

Literacy activities built upon the concept of a spiral framework can easily be introduced to parents at literacy fun nights or other parent meetings that are imple-

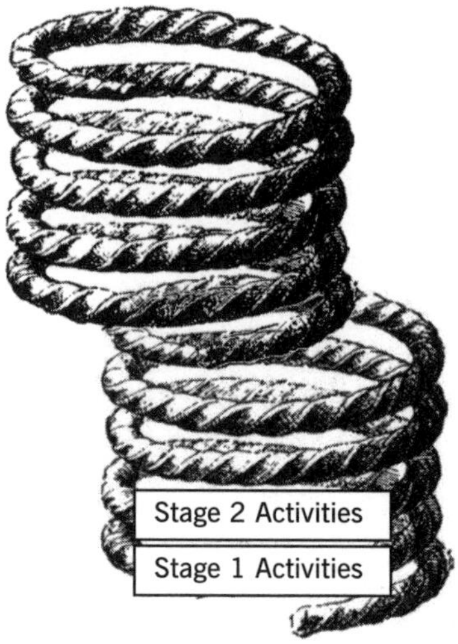

FIGURE 5.5. Sample spiral framework.

mented as part of your school's literacy partnership program. Since we know that there are sequential and predictable reading and writing behaviors all children demonstrate as they move from a prereader to a beginning reader to an independent reader, activities designed around a spiral framework will allow parents to foster the reading development of their children at each stage of development. For the purposes of defining our spiral framework, we have identified four stages of reading development. The characteristics, expected grade levels, and appropriate activities for home, which were developed by reading specialists Terri McCaughan and Lorri Wall, can be found in Tables 5.1 through 5.4. These tables have been provided as a means of helping building administrators facilitate partnerships with families. Frequently, building administrators are asked by parents and community-based organizations (tutorial groups) what they can do to support the school in its efforts to help students fully develop their literacy skills. Many times the question goes unanswered because of the complexity that is involved in providing families and community-based groups with either an approach or a framework that will be beneficial to all involved in the process.

We hope you will find this framework helpful in your efforts to engage both families and community members in your school's literacy program. We would also suggest that you talk with your teachers to determine how they would use this type of framework to enhance their daily literacy instruction in the class. The goal of having such a tool is simply to build instructional capacity that can be connected to students' homes and community in meaningful ways. The school cannot do it alone. However, schools must have in place the structures that will provide pillars of support for the learning that occurs in the classroom.

TABLE 5.1. Stage 1 Reader: Activities for Home

Stage and characteristics	Expected grade levels	Activities

Stage 1: Prereader
• Displays an interest in books
• Recites rhymes and poems
• Is beginning to point to words (left to right, top to bottom)
• Uses pictures in books and own experiences to tell stories
• Can listen and respond to literature
• Begins to retell stories
• Recognizes some words
• Hears likenesses and differences in letter sounds in words (rhyming words, words with shared beginning sounds)
• Knows a few letter names and moves toward recognizing most letter names (uppercase and lowercase)
• Dictates stories from experiences
• Uses pictures, scribbles, letter-like markings, and random letters in writing and moves toward correct letter formation and using initial consonants for words
	Pre-K–midyear kindergarten	• *Picture sorts.* Children can sort pictures to match those that:
		  • rhyme,
		  • have the same beginning sound, and/or
		  • have the same ending sound.
		• *Pattern books.* Read books that have a predictable pattern or rhyme such as *Brown Bear, Brown Bear* by Eric Carle.
		• *Books on tape.* To build concepts about print and vocabulary, listen to books on tape while traveling.
		• *Tell me a story.* Learning the concept and structure of stories is an important first step in learning to read. Read familiar and favorite stories to your child and have them retell the story to you in their own words. Listen for the key events at the beginning, middle, and end of the story as well as details about characters and setting.
		• *A star is born.* Children of this age love to dramatize favorite stories. Encourage your young reader to act out scenes from a story or play by assuming the role of their favorite character. This is not only fun but also helps develop a strong sense of story and vocabulary skills.
		• *Letter identification.* Learning the names of the letters of the alphabet is an important part of being a prereader. Start by introducing letters to your child that they see often, such as those in their name, family member names, and print in the environment (street names and names of favorite restaurants). Don't introduce all letters at one time or letters that are similar like *b* and *d* or *l* and *L*.
		• *Hidden letters.* Ask your child to hunt for letters of the alphabet on boxes and cans of food and household supplies. For example, send your child on a treasure hunt to find five *A*'s, three *B*'s, etc.
		• *Disappearing letters.* Use a bucket of water and a paint brush to let your child practice writing letters of the alphabet outside on the driveway or sidewalk. Encourage your child to quickly name the letter as they write before the letter disappears.
		• *Tactile experiences.* Use materials such as sand, salt, paint, and shaving cream to allow your child to feel the shapes of letters. Experimenting with letter formation using their sense of touch will help young children distinguish between the different features of the letters.

(continued)

TABLE 5.1. *(continued)*

Stage and characteristics	Expected grade levels	Activities
		• *Label it.* Your child's bedroom can become the first place he/she learns to read. Pick one object every few days and write that word on a piece of paper. Tape the paper to the object as a name/label. Your child will quickly learn that print contains a message and will also begin building a sight word vocabulary. • *Purposeful writing.* Even though your child's writing may look like scribbles to you, he/she knows exactly what the message says! Provide chalkboards, a family message board, and a variety of paper so your child can help write messages, invitations, and lists. This will help your child learn that real writers write regularly to communicate a message. • *The magic of magnets.* Magnetic letters can be used on doors, the refrigerator, or even a cookie sheet for children to practice sorting. Children can sort by letters or beginning sounds. For example, "Find all of the *C*'s and put them over here," "Find the letter that makes the sound you hear at the beginning of the word *bus.*" Parents can make simple words for children to read such as the child's name, *mom, dad, dog*, etc. • *Word knowledge.* As you read to your child, point to each word so your child learns that there is a voice-to-print match. Ask your child to point to known words such as those labeled in his/her bedroom or the environment. Books with large print and two or fewer lines of print are best to start with.

DON'T WAIT, START EARLY

The earlier you can start building partnerships for your school-based literacy programs, the better. Because of the demands of the day-to-day operations of meeting the needs of the students who walk the halls of your school, it is easy to overlook the opportunity of building intervention and prevention partnership programs at the earliest possible stage. Persons who may be indirectly connected to your school community but who will soon enter into parenthood or who are indirectly connected as day care providers can benefit from structured sessions on literacy readiness emphasizing what parents and day care providers can do to support literacy development.

This school of thought is different from sessions that would solely focus on why early literacy is important. Perhaps we have sufficiently informed the larger community of the importance of early literacy development. What we have not mastered is the engagement of those individuals with literacy development activities, resources, and training on how to use the resources that enhance literacy development with toddlers and infants.

TABLE 5.2. Stage 2 Reader: Activities for Home

Stage and characteristics	Expected grade levels	Activities
Stage 2: Beginning reader • Can point to words when reading • Adds to sight word recognition • Reads simple text (one or two lines) smoothly • Uses knowledge of word families to read and write new words (*at, cat, fat*) • Begins to recognize blends and digraphs such as: *th, sh, ch,* and *wh* • Uses beginning sounds to figure out unknown words in reading • Continues to use pictures and own experiences to read • Begins to correct reading errors more consistently using meaning and visual cues • Predicts what will happen next in stories • Understands the story when reading and is able to answer questions	Midyear kindergarten–midyear first grade	• *Phonics.* As your child learns to decode new words, spend a few minutes each day practicing this. As you and your child look at a new word, touch each letter and say the sound, moving from left to right through the word (for example, say the sounds /r/ /u/ /n/ and blend the sounds to make *run*). Begin with short, easy words such as *pop, sat,* or *log.* With words that contain a smaller "chunk," show your child how to find the smaller part of the word to help them read. For example, your child might not know the word *flat,* but they may know the word *at.* This part of the word will help them decode the new and unknown word. • *Word games.* Play a word game with your child by writing high-frequency words on cards. Place the cards upside down in a stack and take turns choosing a card and blending the sounds to form the word. You can use the word in a sentence to make sure your child understands the meaning. • *Word sorts.* Children at this stage begin adding to the bank of words they know by sight. Charts or lists can be started at home on the refrigerator or the back of a door to allow children to sort words and develop concepts. You can start developing lists by categories such as *Food Words, Animal Words,* and *Household Words* and then move to more challenging lists such as *Action Words, Describing Words,* or words with *–ing.* • *Magnetic words.* Magnetic letters can be used as students experiment with making new words from known words. Children can make the word *nap,* for example, and change the beginning or ending letter to make new words. This is a great way to help students practice adding endings to words such as *-s, -ed, -er,* and *-ing.* • *Tactile experiences.* Use materials such as sand, salt, paint, and shaving cream to allow children to feel the shapes of the letters and words. Experimenting with making words in a variety of ways is interesting for children.

(conntinued)

TABLE 5.2. *(continued)*

Stage and characteristics	Expected grade levels	Activities
• Uses beginning sounds when writing and moves toward representing more sounds with the correct letter • Writes a complete sentence and is beginning to leave spaces between words • Moves toward writing multiple sentences on one topic • Uses capital letters and ending punctuation • Writes high-frequency words independently		• *Story talk.* As you read aloud to your child pause occasionally to think aloud about the story. You can say: "I wonder what's going to happen next!" You can ask a question: "Do you know what a palace is?" or you can point out: "Look where the little mouse is now." Talking about stories with your children allows them to develop their vocabulary, make connections to real-world experiences, and use what they know about the world to make predictions, draw conclusions, and figure out new words. • *Write on.* Use children's drawings, photographs they have taken, or pictures in magazines in order to help children generate a complete sentence. As children process, they can begin adding details to their sentence. • *Fluent writing.* Your child is beginning to learn how to write many words by memory. Play a game with your child by setting a timer to one minute and seeing how many words he or she can write by memory. Chart your child's progress and encourage him or her to try to beat their own score each week. • *Practice makes perfect.* Your child will become a better reader with more opportunities to practice. Make sure that you have a good selection of reading material at your child's reading level so that he or she can read every day. It will be fun for students to read to older or younger siblings, grandparents, or even neighbors!

While expecting a child is exciting, it can be and is often overwhelming for soon-to-be parents. There are many aspects to preparing for the arrival of a newborn, which range from getting the nursery ready for the arrival to determining who is going to be the child's pediatrician, not to mention the psychological adaptation that parents encounter. Many of these parenting challenges and the others that we have not mentioned are unanticipated and they become masked by the natural excitement of parenthood. For the first time, parents of newborns find themselves having to make personal sacrifices in order to ensure the well-being of their child. This in itself becomes an eye opener and requires an adjustment period.

These challenges create unique opportunities for parents. Some, for the first time, find themselves overwhelmed with the need to strike a balance between commitments within and outside the home and making certain that they spend the necessary time holding, cuddling, and bonding with their newborn, giving the child a sense of security that he or she needs. On the other hand, parents must ensure that they maximize those earlier years of language development. We

(text continues on p. 148)

TABLE 5.3. Stage 3 Reader: Activities for Home

Stage and characteristics	Expected grade levels	Activities
Stage 3: Transitional reader • Quickly chunks words into parts to figure out unknown words • Searches for information in the book (checks the picture, searches through the words, rereads to check for meaning) • Is fluent and expressive when reading new text • Understands the story or important parts when reading • Makes connections when reading stories and likes to read about the same characters (series books) • Continues to expand high-frequency words in reading and writing • Includes a beginning, middle, and end when writing stories • Hears sounds in sequence and moves toward correct spellings of words • Uses descriptive words in sentences • Likes to write independent of the teacher or parent	Midfirst grade–beginning second grade	• *Context clues.* Sometimes children can figure out an unknown word by using other words in the sentence and what they know about how words work. Help your child with this strategy by reminding him or her to ask, "Does the word make sense here?" and "Does it sound right" and "Does it look right?" • *Expression.* Reading with expression is an important part of reading fluency and is shown to lead to a better understanding of text. Have your child practice reading an easy story or play to you. Show your child how to read it and make it sound as though the people are really talking. • *Old favorites.* Your child is able to read stories at increasing levels of difficulties. This is the perfect time to get your child hooked on easy chapter books or books with a recurring character. Series like Frog and Toad by Arnold Lobel and Junie B. Jones by Barbara Park are favorites. Children will love reading about their favorite characters! • *Word games.* By now your child should have a large bank of high-frequency words that he or she knows automatically, and your child should be adding three to five words each week to this core bank of words. Write high-frequency words on cards and as a family play Go Fish or Concentration. • *Magnetic letters.* Ask children to make longer words with multiple syllables. • *Read with me.* It is still important to read to your child, but equally as important to listen to your child read to you. Take turns reading. You may read the first page and then ask your child to read the next page. If your child gets stuck on a word have him or her stretch through the word using what he or she knows about letter sounds, and always ask if his or her choice looks right and makes sense in the sentence. • *Picture stories.* Help your child select three to six pictures from magazines or newspapers and put them together to tell a story. Your child can number the pictures and tell or write the story. This is great for developing creativity and for building vocabulary and oral language skills. • *Notes of love.* Place a small note of love and encouragement in your child's pocket, lunchbox, or book bag. Your child will enjoy reading the notes and will see the many purposes for writing! • *Letter writing.* An excellent way to begin to have children generate multiple sentences on a topic is to have them write a letter to a family member or friend. Ask the people who receive the notes to respond if possible. • *Comic strip writing.* Use pictures from comic strips or comic books as a springboard for having your child write an original story.

TABLE 5.4. Stages 4 Reader: Activities for Home

Stage and characteristics	Expected grade levels	Activities
Stage 4: Independent reader • Reads books at increasing levels of difficulty with speed, accuracy, and expression • Reads a variety of genres for multiple purposes (plays, informational texts, articles, narratives, biographies, legends) • Reads longer stories and chapter books with rich vocabulary • Uses multiple strategies simultaneously to cope with the challenges of more difficult texts • Integrates word recognition and comprehension strategies automatically • Skims text quickly to retrieve information and make inferences • Begins to add details to written stories and paragraphs • Begins to become interested in writing for a variety of purposes • Vocabulary becomes more precise and descriptive • Uses correct spelling for frequently used word	Beginning second grade–fifth grade	• *Journals.* Keeping a journal is one way for your child to write down daily events and record his or her thoughts. Help your child start a journal by discussing topics that can be written about, such as moving to a new house, making a new friend, or a review of the latest movie you saw as a family. Keep a journal yourself and compare topics and notes at the end of the week. • *Treasure hunts.* Students love to hunt for information based on clues. Design easy treasure hunts using the reading material found at home, such as the newspaper or telephone book. Have your child hunt for the information you would need if you wanted to send flowers to a sick friend, find a good movie to see, or if you needed someone to repair your car or home appliance. Treasure hunts are a great way to reinforce the many purposes for reading. • *Compare–contrast.* Comparing how things are similar and different is a high-level thinking skill that enhances a child's ability to interact with text in a meaningful way. At home, children can be given the opportunity to compare and contrast books, movies, vacations, and events. • *What's that word?* We can never teach children all of the words they will need to know in life, but we can certainly add to their vocabulary on a regular basis. As a family, choose a word for the week that is interesting or unusual. Children can make predictions about the meaning of the word prior to reading the word in context or locating the word in a dictionary. As a family, make sure to find meaningful ways to use the word in your conversations during the week. • *Answer this.* Readers who can ask good questions as they read usually have a good understanding of the text. As part of your family reading time, allow your child to jot down questions for you to answer from a story you are sharing together. This will provide a chance for you to interact with your child while reading and also letting your child practice those important questioning skills. • *Mystery ending.* Have your child read the first part of a story or article and then write the end on his or her own. After writing his or her own ending, he or she can read and compare the ending with the author's ending. • *Comprehension games.* Good readers use several different comprehension strategies to make meaning from text. Current research points to the use of several strategies that effective readers use, including the five that follow.

(continued)

TABLE 5.4. *(continued)*

Stage and characteristics	Expected grade levels	Activities
		The names of all five strategies can be written on index cards. As you read with your child, have him or her pick a card and show you how to use the strategy to better understand what you are reading. Your child will benefit from you playing too! • *Creating mental images.* This is the process of creating pictures or images while reading. Mental images can include sights, sounds, smells, tastes, sensations, and emotions. Good readers form mental images to help them understand, remember, and enjoy reading material. To help your child create mental images, help him or her to remember to use the following sentence starters: "When I read this, I imagine. . .," "This makes me feel. . .," "When I read this part, I could almost smell the. . . .," • *Making inferences.* Not everything communicated in reading material is directly or clearly stated. Good readers use their prior knowledge and the information in the book to understand implied meanings. Readers take what they know and gather clues from the reading material and think ahead to make a judgment. The following questions can help your child with inferential thinking skills: "What lesson did you learn?" "What is the author trying to tell us?" "What caused this to happen?" • *Questioning.* Good readers wonder and ask questions to focus their reading and clarify meaning. They wonder what the reading material is about before they read and they make guesses or predictions about what is happening while they read. They also ask questions after they read to see if they have understood the reading material. To foster good questioning skills, help your child get in the habit of asking these types of questions: "How come. . .?" "Why did. . .?" "I'm wondering . . . and now I know. . . ." • *Determining importance.* Noticing important ideas in reading material helps readers identify information that is essential to know and remember. Readers must know the difference between less important information and key ideas that are most important for understanding the reading material. Finding the important details while reading can be practiced by helping your child ask these questions: "Why am I reading this?" "How is this text organized?" "What does this seem to be mostly about?" "What are the major points?" • *Making connections.* Readers understand what they read by making connections between their prior knowledge and the new information in the reading material. They can connect what they are reading to their own lives, another story they have read, or something in the world. Have your child use the following sentence starters as you discuss books to help him or her make connections: "This reminds me of. . ." "This makes me think of. . ." "This is helping me. . ."

all know that during the earlier years of a child's development the brain is very much like a sponge. It is during this period of that we stand the greatest chance of preventing language deficiencies versus trying to fix language delays in later years.

Early Intervention

While schools cannot take on all aspects of childhood development, we can take on a few things that will yield success. The ground is fertile in the area of early literacy development, and you will find that your focus and efforts will make a difference. The research suggests that we have large numbers of students who are entering school as kindergartners with deficits in the area of literacy (National Research Council, 1998). Some of the contributing factors are:

1. The words that are spoken in the home; in particular, the types of conversations that are held with the child in the home setting, or the lack of child and adult conversation.
2. The amount of time the child spends watching television.
3. The number of appropriate books that children have access to in the home that pique their interest.
4. How much time and attention the parent can give to the child during the day.
5. How much and whether the parent(s) read.

All of these factors and so many more impact language development and contribute to how ready students are when they enter the doors of the school building for the first time.

Children whose parents may not have provided them with opportunities to enhance their literacy development do not know where or how to get started. While everyone wants all children to succeed, gaining access to the resources or knowing how to use the resources creates barriers for parents and day care providers.

If at all possible, do not wait until students arrive to begin the process of teaching certain skills. In particular, we know that children in their earlier months of development begin to develop a foundation for what will become a springboard for their initial reading success, known as emergent literacy. Sulzby and Teale (1996) explain that "emergent literacy" is concerned with the earliest phases of literacy development, the period between birth and the time when children read and write conventionally. The term emergent literacy signals a belief that, in a literate society, young children—even 1- and 2-year-olds—are in the process of becoming literate" (p. 730).

Yet, our partnership support systems often do not begin with families until after the student is enrolled as a preschooler or a kindergartner in our schools.

Many of the challenges that our middle and high school students, and even some adults, struggle with today in the areas of reading fluency and comprehension stem from problems that could have been addressed earlier in life had an early intervention been in place (National Research Council, 1998).

A starting point for this type of partnership could be as simple as asking preschool teachers and kindergarten teachers to brainstorm a list of skills that students should know when they enter school. Based on each identified skill, teachers could provide activities and ways an adult could engage the child in developing particular skills and the repetition (frequency) that is needed. To take it a step further, teachers could also identify the skills and possible activities that could be used with the children by an adult in a home setting and create early literacy packets to give to parents-to-be or day care providers.

Given the complexity of language development, we would encourage principals to conduct one or more mini-workshops in the use of the resources. This type of effort should not be done in isolation. Principals may want to consider forming an early literacy team and asking them to brainstorm ideas regarding the development of this type of intervention and prevention outreach program. The variety of ideas that will more than likely be generated will help to ensure that the program and resources that will be developed will address the needs of a diverse parent and community population.

We cannot forget that, just as our students have different needs, so will families. A goal for a program of this nature would be to include parents and others as early partners and facilitators in literacy development as well as to empower them with the knowledge and resources they will need to give children a stronger start. This goal is predicated on the reality that families and others who make up the support system for the children have a very important role in helping the children to successfully transition into a more formal educational environment.

21ST-CENTURY LEARNING PARTNERSHIP OPPORTUNITIES

Technology plays an important role in the development of extended learning partnerships. The old adage "nothing remains the same but change" is as true today for principals and schools as in previous years.

Technology may very well challenge principals to think outside of the box. Let's begin this discussion from the standpoint of how technological connectivity has changed the face of our local communities and world. Thomas Freidman said it best: "the world is flat."

In his book *The World Is Flat: A Brief History of the Twenty-First Century*, Friedman (2005) ventures to dissect globalization and how we as a world have become, and will continue to become, more and more interdependent. Consider that just 10 years ago a blackberry was known only as a type of wild fruit, and wikkies, emoticons, texting, Myspace, and Facebook were not a part of the modern vocabulary. Today, it is possible to have a conversation with someone on the other side of the world without ever leaving your computer. Worldwide use of the Internet has made communication and information gathering available at phenomenal speed.

With that in mind, it is important to realize that students today were born into a world that is different from 10 years ago, and we can hardly imagine how different it will be in the next 10 years. In order for all students to have equitable opportunities to participate in a world that is quickly and vastly changing, we must ensure that they have the fundamental skills—a starting place is a strong literacy foundation.

At this point, we would agree that most students are technologically savvy. They know how to download their music from the Internet, text message their friends at the speed of lightning, create wikkies, websites on Myspace, and blogs. It is amazing to observe students actively engaged in classrooms that allow them to use technology beyond the basics of creating PowerPoint presentations and spreadsheets.

While these skills are needed, our students' abilities far exceed the basics of creating classroom presentations. They are *digital natives*, the first generation to grow up with technology, surrounded by video games, MP3 players, camera (cell) phones, and YouTube. Meanwhile, many of us are considered *digital immigrants*, that is, we have learned to adapt to and use technology. We may still revert, however, to our old ways, by calling to ask if someone received our e-mail Prensky, 2001). Perhaps this is why we have not realized how powerful technology and 21st-century learning environments could be in the realm of literacy partnership structures and programs.

Some examples of 21st-century use of technology to promote literacy include the following:

- *Webcasting*. Create literacy modules that can be accessed via the Internet. These webcasts could serve as tutorials for the student and the parent to reinforce literacy skills. The teacher could model for parents strategies to be used at home. This would place partnership opportunities at your fingertips twenty-four hours a day, seven days a week.
- *MP3 players*. Students could download books onto their MP3 players, or the teacher could provide recordings that can be loaded onto MP3 players for vocabulary development.
- *WWW resources*. Provide families with the many free resources available on the World Wide Web. In addition, there is free software available for schools to download and create their own tutorial sessions and launch them for the community to access.

ENGLISH LANGUAGE LEARNERS: REACHING OUT

As the building principal, in addition to technological considerations, it is also necessary to recognize other important pillars associated with 21st-century learning, including globalization and diversity. In order for our communities and our country to succeed in the future, we must do more to address these issues in our schools as we prepare all students to function in a global market.

Establishing partnerships with families of ELLs as a part of your school's partnership program can yield great success, especially in the area of literacy development and communication. As with all partnerships, trust is the starting point. When parents and/or guardians know that schools have their child's best interest as their objective, there is a foundation upon which the school can begin to build the partnership.

The principal may want to initiate planning by meeting with the school's ELL teacher and perhaps the district's ELL supervisor for ideas and suggestions in reaching out to parents of ELLs. Often we think that one has to reinvent the wheel, it is not necessary to start from ground zero.

Another strategy should include contacting other principals and districts that have successful programs for the parents of ELL students. This contact may provide insight into best practices and other ideas that will guide the strategies and thought processes for your school's literacy partnership. As with all partnerships, determine what the goals are for the partnership and then identify strategies that will facilitate the literacy partnership with parents of ELLs.

Some ideas to keep on the radar when developing literacy partnerships follow. It is important to remember that literacy partnerships with parents of English language learners should be integrated into the school's overall partnership program and not exist as a stand-alone program. It should be seamless, yet purposefully directed and focused in order to for families to benefit from the school's efforts.

- Reach out to parents of ELLs.
- Enlist parent coordinators to assist with the formation of the partnerships.
- Determine the need for translators and other services that will assist with the literacy partnership.
- Build an ELL parent resource center within the school.
- Ensure that the literacy outreach partnership programs are culturally rich.
- Include literacy resources for parents of ELLs.
- Establish a Luggage for Learning community-based partnership as described earlier in this chapter.

- Ensure that early literacy efforts facilitate services and opportunities to partner with parents of ELLs.
- Create opportunities to remain current in this area.

DRIVERS AND INHIBITORS

Prior to beginning any new initiative, it is always useful to identify factors that will move the initiative forward and factors that may impede the initiative. Table 5.5 lists some *drivers* and *inhibitors* that may affect the successful implementation of your literacy partnership program. Spending time brainstorming potential drivers and inhibitors that may be specific to the school and community will be time well spent. Knowing the road blocks or obstacles prior to implementation will also help during the planning process.

Remember, engaging the community is more than a notion. It must be well thought out and planned—a process. Proper planning and fiscal responsibility are important in gaining the trust of potential partners.

Literacy is a foundational building block upon which our students will grow academically. Therefore, it is important to ensure that the literacy foundation is instructionally sound, age-appropriate, and well planned and organized. Involve as many people as possible who make up the circle of influence for your students, bring together a representative team, devise an action plan, develop or select a current literacy program that meets the needs of your specific student population,

TABLE 5.5. Drivers and Inhibitors

Drivers	Inhibitors
• Staff support	• Lack of staff support
• Literacy framework/program	• Lack of parental and community participation
• Well-defined partnerships	• Insufficient financial resources
• Community support	• Inadequate or nonexistent training
• Parental support	• Fragmented program
• Adequate training	• Language barriers
• Communication plan	• Time commitments
• Volunteers (e.g., interpreters)	• Lack of trust in the school
• Financial resources	• Insufficient data
• Relationships	• Differing expectations
• Effective use of data	• Politics
• Focus	

infuse 21st-century technology, be aware of the drivers and inhibitors, and ensure that there is an evaluation and adjustment mechanism built into the program.

CONCLUSIONS

This chapter has discussed the importance of reaching out to parents and the community in order to have the best chance for success in a literacy program. In addition to discussing some of the research rationale, we looked at the notion of circles of influence. Steps leading up to an action plan include identifying the stakeholders, determining the levels of responsibility that are required, and determining the people and financial resources that are needed. After discussing a few partnership programs, the discussion focused on various communication methods and sample activities that can be provided in home-school programs.

LOOKING AHEAD

Chapter 6 will focus on the need to have an effective evaluation system for teachers that relies not just on formal measures but also informal measures. Evaluation is one of the most important responsibilities that we, as principals, have, yet it is one that is often the most uncomfortable. Our final chapter will help provide a framework for evaluation and describe the use of portfolios to enhance any evaluation system.

CHAPTER 6

KNOWING YOUR STAFF

> The secret of joy in work is contained in one word—excellence. To know how to do something well is to enjoy it.
>
> —PEARL S. BUCK (1964)

National, and in many instances, statewide, initiatives underscore the need for effective literacy instruction in our schools. We know that literacy is the foundation for overall learning and should be structured and strong. How can building administrators evaluate their staff to ensure that they are implementing strong literacy instruction? Do they attempt to use a one-size-fits-all evaluative instrument?

Often evaluation systems rely solely on one process for all teaching personnel, whether they are classroom teachers, guidance counselors, or reading specialists. There are severe limitations in this approach, specifically in its role in improving the quality of teaching and learning, and more important, improving student achievement. One or more hour-long classroom observations during the academic year by a building administrator provides only a glimpse of a teacher's skills and abilities—and only a fragment of the full range of responsibilities and activities in which the teacher is routinely engages.

For the literacy specialist, a supervision model that relies solely on classroom observation will lead to artificial, misleading, and incomplete portraits of the specialists' performance. More important, this approach will limit the principal's ability to fully evaluate the specialist. This approach will neither contribute to continuous school improvement nor improve student achievement. Using different approaches has become more imperative in the light of various school reform efforts.

One Principal's Awakening

We vividly recall the turning point in one principal's career. Six months into her first year as a principal she realized that she was not leading the instructional efforts, but being led by the sequence of events that were occurring in her building. Her challenge entailed striking balance between handling the day-to-day affairs of the school, which ranged from resolving bus discipline issues to managing personnel situations to observing classroom teachers. As an administrator, one would conclude, "This is not what being an instructional leader involves." However, she believed that eventually there would be a breakthrough in which all of the other demands would somehow either cease or go away. During one of her conferences with her supervisor, she was asked questions that required responses as an instructional leader:

What trends do you see in your reading data?

Are the trends unique to one teacher or the entire grade level?

What strategies do you think will yield the best results for your students?

For what are you willing to hold yourself accountable?

What tools will allow you to help teachers understand the strengths and weaknesses of their instruction?

This became an awakening moment for her because she realized that in order to address the student achievement and instructional needs, she was required to become an *instructional leader,* not just an operations manager. She also realized that the district teacher evaluation tool was not going to help her determine the quality of the instructional program at her school. She chose to accept the challenge and the conversation as an opportunity to become an instructional leader.

Her choice ultimately led to some great discoveries. One of these discoveries was that quality teaching and learning entails more than one's willingness; it also requires the principal to use a system that will allow one to define best practices, observe best practices, and monitor best practices. Based on this reality, we worked toward the development of a supplemental evaluation system that would enable her and other principals to know what to look for to effectively gauge instructional delivery in the classroom.

Principals and administrators often find themselves facing challenges similar to the situation described in this case study when trying to develop a strong literacy program. They may find that they are being led by literacy circumstances—such as students reading below grade level, students lacking emergent literacy skills, or teachers who do not have the necessary literacy training—rather than providing instructional focus. The need for this focus, however, has never been more important.

THE IMPERATIVE OF EDUCATIONAL REFORM

The challenge of educating all students is viewed by educators as formidable, but possible. Teaching and learning is a complex process that reflects the influence of teachers, parents, and community members. Layered onto this complex process is the abundance of mandates that demand focus and attention. Over the past ten to fifteen years, school principals have had to define, juggle, and, in many cases, lead a variety of initiatives to address the increasing demands of school reform. With each new reform effort, there has been increased accountability as well as new standards and mandates. Within each reform effort, there has also been an emphasis on the need for highly qualified teachers and staff for the nation's schools. Teacher evaluation, in this context, has become more critical than ever before.

A Nation at Risk

In 1983, The National Commission on Excellence in Education released a report entitled A Nation at Risk: The Imperative for Educational Reform. This report could be considered the beginning of the reform efforts in education. The report forwarded several recommendations that began to drive many educational decision-making processes. *A Nation at Risk* indicated our schools were "generally encouraging mediocre and undemanding work and that much more intellectually challenging instruction would be needed to make students more academically and economically competitive" (Cohen, 1995, p. 740). The report made it clear that the failure of America's educational system was planted squarely at the feet of school administrators (Cassell, 1999).

While one might agree that, on the surface, the recommendations appeared genuine in nature, this report also initiated doubts about our public schools and their leadership. *A Nation At Risk* outlined the following recommendations:

- Graduation requirements should be strengthened so that all students establish a foundation in five basics: English, mathematics, science, social studies, and computer science.
- Schools and colleges should adopt higher and measurable standards for academic performance.
- The amount of time students spend engaged in learning should be significantly increased.
- *The teaching profession should be strengthened through standards for preparation and professional growth* (NCREL, 2004).

Goals 2000

On the heels of *A Nation at Risk*, President George H. W. Bush introduced America 2000. The program was renamed Goals 2000 under the Clinton administration. The Goals 2000: Educate America Act was passed by Congress in March of 1994 (Ohanian, 2000). Although Goals 2000 was ambitious in nature, the goals created another framework for public education that focused on rigorous and in some cases demanding academic standards and assessments (Cohen, 1995).

The Goals 2000 Act legalized its six original education goals as well as two new goals in the areas of professional development and parental involvement. The goals specifically stated that, by the year 2000:

- All children in the United States will start school ready to learn.
- The high school graduation rate will increase to at least 90%.
- All students will leave grades 4, 8, and 12 having demonstrated competency over challenging subject matter, including English, mathematics, science, foreign languages, civics and government, economics, the arts, history, and geography, and every school in America will ensure that all students learn to use their minds well, so they may be prepared for responsible citizenship, further learning, and productive employment in our nation's modern economy.
- U.S. students will be first in the world in mathematics and science achievement.
- Every adult in the United States will be literate and will possess the knowledge and skills necessary to compete in a global economy and exercise the rights and responsibilities of citizenship.
- Every school in the United States will be free of drugs, violence, and the unauthorized presence of firearms and alcohol and will offer a disciplined environment conducive to learning.
- The nation's teaching force will have access to programs for the continued improvement of their professional skills and the opportunity to acquire the knowledge and skills needed to instruct and prepare all American students for the next century.
- Every school will promote partnerships that will increase parental involvement and participation in promoting the social, emotional, and academic growth of children (Ohanian, 2000).

While this act attempted to more closely align standards, curriculum, assessment, and instruction, it was viewed by educational leaders as another voice of reform that once again told practitioners what they needed to do as they educated young people. This movement was not viewed as a powerful national movement but was seen as a politicians' reform movement (Cohen, 1995). Yet, Goals 2000 was interpreted as a way of reforming the entire educational system rather than a method of improving the system. In other words, Goals 2000 was a way to change the educational system, not necessarily to make it better. Goals 2000 was amended in 1996 and its reign ended unfulfilled in 2001 after the change in presidential leadership.

No Child Left Behind

Not long after Goals 2000 was put to rest, President George W. Bush introduced the No Child Left Behind (NCLB) Act, which was signed into law on January 8, 2002. The tenets of this law are to ensure that every child succeeds academically. NCLB affects virtually every program authorized under the Elementary and Secondary Education Act (ESEA). ESEA Programs include Title I, improving teacher quality, initiatives for Limited English Proficient (LEP) students, and safe and drug-free schools (National School Boards Association, 2002).

The NCLB requirements fall into three primary areas: testing and accountability, employment and hiring practices, and choices for parents. There are also a variety of miscellaneous provisions. The goals of the act state the following:

- All students will reach high standards, at a minimum attaining proficiency or better in reading and mathematics by 2013–2014.
- All limited English proficient students will become proficient in English.
- By 2005–2006, all students will be taught by highly qualified teachers (revised March 2004).
- All students will be educated in learning environments that are safe, drug-free and conducive to learning.
- All students will graduate from high school (Virginia Department of Education, 2009).

Critics of NCLB have suggested that the act does not take into account the many cultural and diverse educational settings of each school district. They argue that NCLB pigeonholes schools and students into two groups—those who pass and those who do not (Schloss, 2004). One superintendent lamented that, under the rating system of the NCLB, district schools that had received national and state awards for student achievement would be labeled as "needing improvement" (Schloss, 2004).

Regardless of the reform movement, it is worthy to note that teacher performance and evaluation is a strand in each movement. Clearly, those most interested in reform have seen the need to ensure that we have highly qualified teachers working with our students. In this context, knowing the strengths and needs of our staff members becomes paramount, especially in the area of literacy.

WHAT DOES RESEARCH TELL US?

Research is clear that effective teaching provides an invaluable key to improving education and that systematic, effective evaluation of teachers is essential to assuring effective teaching. (Shinkfield & Stufflebeam, 1995). There have been many problems with teacher evaluations, however, due to the lack of agreement on what constitutes good teaching and due to the focus on accountability rather than improved performance. Perhaps because of these problems, educators have made more efforts to improve teacher evaluation by developing better systems.

The Joint Committee on Standards for Educational Evaluation is a committee representing 16 organizations, including the National Association of Elementary School Principals, the National Education Association, and the National School Boards Association. This committee has identified four major standards that all personnel evaluation systems should meet (Joint Committee on Standards for Educational Evaluation, 2007).

- *Propriety* standards require that evaluations be conducted ethically and legally with appropriate regard and respect for the personnel involved.
- *Utility* standards are used to guide the evaluation process so that they will be informative, timely, and influential.
- *Feasibility* standards ensure that evaluation systems are as easy to implement as possible without undue time or resources expended.
- *Accuracy* standards require that the information gleaned from the evaluation be accurate and reliable, without undue bias.

Colby, Bradshaw, and Joyner (2002) identified several criteria for more effective evaluation systems: linking evaluation to the school's goals, using a variety of data, having appropriate feedback mechanisms, and involving teachers in a meaningful way in the process. This approach views teacher evaluation within an organizational framework. The framework includes school climate, instructional leadership of the principal, professional development, and student learning. (National Association of State Boards of Education, 2000).

Numerous researchers have supported using multiple sources of data collection in evaluations as one way to address the accuracy standards of the Joint Committee (Grady, 1992; Stronge & Helm, 1991; Valencia, Hiebert, & Afflerbach 1994). Peterson (1995) summed up the rationale for using multiple data sources with two primary reasons: (1) the limited nature of just one source and (2) the satisfaction of a need to address teachers' diverse responsibilities. Many researchers have noted that reports of teacher performance based on one or two classroom visits are often inaccurate and unreliable. Many sources of data in addition to classroom visits are available for consideration, including a portfolio, walk-throughs, observation outside the classroom, peer evaluation, self-evaluation, client surveys, and artifacts such as student work, lesson plans, student reports, teacher tests, documentation of professional activity, and student achievement.

Tucker and Stronge (2005) support this concept by stating that it is important to develop an evaluation system that will fairly and reasonably assess teachers' success with students. For Tucker and Stronge, this approach requires an ongoing system of data collection that is built into the school culture.

Researchers have also confirmed that a single, one-form-for-all approach would not be equitable or effective in the evaluation of teaching staff. In addition to using multiple sources of data, Stronge and Tucker (2005) suggest that teachers and specialists should have an evaluation system that recognizes their different responsibilities. A primary way to differentiate evaluation systems is in the Goals and Roles model that Stronge and Tucker propose. In this model, evaluation is built around specific job responsibilities and performance indicators that delineate clear expectations for teachers and specialists.

A good source for more information about teacher evaluation and current practices is the website: *www.teacherevaluation.net*.

SUPPLEMENTING THE EXISTING EVALUATION SYSTEM

Principals and their staff members should consider developing a supplemental system that defines what good literacy instruction is and clearly delineates the desired performance measures for staff. There is much evidence to suggest that providing literacy teachers and specialists with a supplemental system will allow the building administrator to determine a more comprehensive picture of the specialists' performance. A supplemental system that reflects the roles and responsibilities practiced by both classroom teachers and literacy specialists adds context to the teacher evaluation process. Teachers and specialists must be involved in the development of this system so that it is meaningful to them.

Use a Committee

The use of a committee consisting of literacy specialists/coaches, teachers, parents, media specialists, and others is invaluable. Members of the committee could begin by brainstorming effective teaching and learning literacy strategies that should be visible in classrooms. If there is a school literacy team, the process can be incorporated as a function of this team and not as a separate evaluation team.

Having members of the staff engaged in a discussion about evaluation will help to break the traditional mindset that the administrator possesses a "magic wand" of all instructional knowledge. While there will be myriad ideas concerning what literacy instruction should look like, these many ideas should not impede the process. Varying thoughts and suggestions will certainly surface as group members seek to find their place in the group.

Group dynamics theorist Tuckman (1965, 2001) suggests that groups go through several stages before reaching the "performing" stage and that groups need to go through these stages in order to be effective.

- *Forming*. During this stage, there is more dependence on the leader for guidance and direction. The leader must be prepared to answer a lot of questions about the purpose of the group. Group members seek acceptance from others while avoiding conflict; focus tends to be on who does what, meeting dates, timelines, and so on. Group members begin to gather information and impressions of each other.
- *Storming*. During the storming phase, decisions do not come easily. Cordialities wear off and confrontations begin. Group members begin to vie for position. While clarity of purpose increases, there are still many uncertainties. Rules to prevent conflict emerge.
- *Norming*. Tasks and responsibilities become clearer and are agreed upon. Group members have a better understanding of each other and an appreciation for one another's views. A cohesive, effective group emerges, with commitment and unity of purpose evident. While there is respect for the leadership, the leadership is also shared within the group. Groups must work hard to reach this stage and resist outside pressure to change.
- *Performing*. The team is more strategically aware of what it is doing and why. There is a shared vision with a focus on their goals. Disagreements are resolved within the team in a positive manner. Interdependence and flexibility are the hallmarks of this stage. Group members know each other well and can work together. All groups do not reach this stage.
- *Adjourning*. This stage was added to Tuckman's original four stages in 1975. In this stage, the group disbands and adjourns their work, because their work is fulfilled. (Neill, 2004)

To assist the committee in moving through these stages as effectively as possible, a mind map can serve as a framework. The mind map is a tool that can improve note taking by quickly identifying the structure of a subject, the relative importance of various points, and the ways they relate to one another. Mind maps can be used to summarize information, think through problems, and present information in a useful format. The map can also be used later as a tool that will enable the principal and others to walk into a classroom and quickly assess the presence or absence of certain items.

Provide Direction to the Committee

Providing the committee with a charge that will keep them focused and energized toward completing the task is critical to the process. For example, within the committee charge, there should be an expression of the need for members to find common ground among their diverse backgrounds. This can be accomplished by articulating areas of responsibility and duties, which will help to ensure that one person does not dominate the process—all voices need to be heard, with buy-in (or at least consensus) from the members of the committee.

Figure 6.1 is a sample planning process for a committee. In this example, after the establishment of the committee, the committee should consider and answer three critical, guiding questions regarding the literacy program:

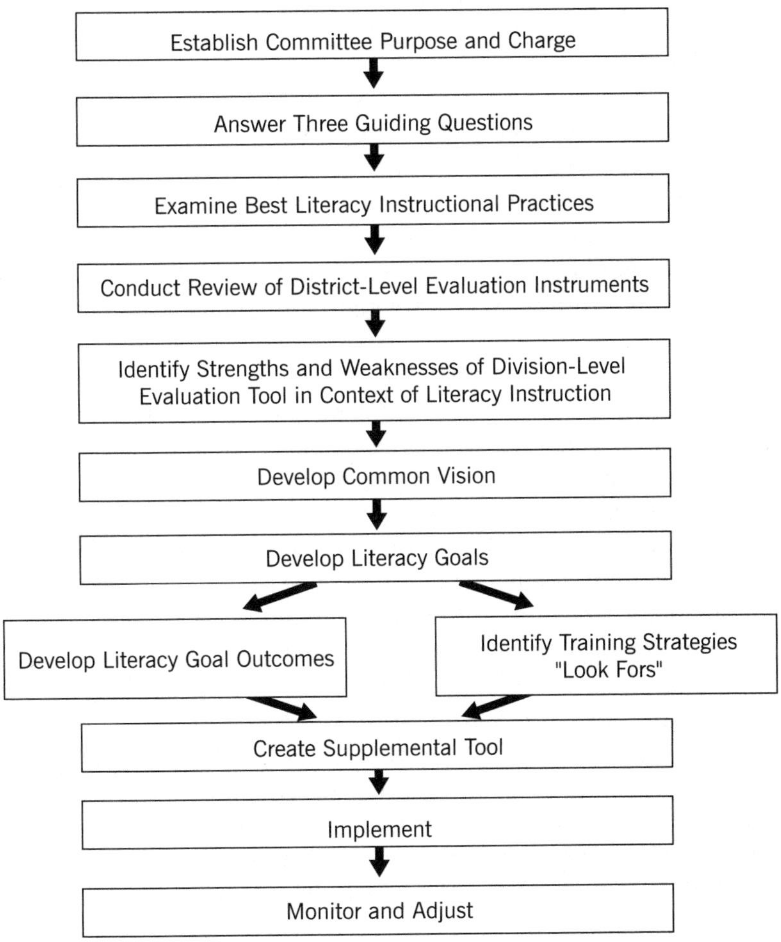

FIGURE 6.1. Planning process.

1. *Why are we evaluating?* Answering this question will help to establish the motive for evaluation and the need for a supplemental evaluation tool.
2. *What are we evaluating?* The answer to this question should help to delineate what components are being considered, the successes expected, and the strategies used to reach those successes.
3. *How are we evaluating?* Determining the answer to this question will help define methods and means of evaluating (Johnson, 2002).

Without the answers to these guiding questions, it would be difficult to determine what needs to be done to gather more information about literacy practices in your school.

Members of the committee should use a consensus model. Simply stated, consensus is a strategy used to ensure that each member of the group will participate in the discussion and support the decision, even though there may be minor areas of disagreement. It is not a majority voting model. A consensus model may take longer, but it is worth the time to have all members of the committee involved. Letting committee members brainstorm what literacy practices should look like, for example, may be a first step. Having them agree on which are the most important strategies for teachers in the building to use might take more time. There are a variety of tools to use to help groups reach consensus. Setting an expectation for consensus is important for the building principal. Why? Because at the end of the process, the principal will want something manageable that the staff will support.

The question that may resonate with principals is this: How can anyone get a diverse committee of individuals to reach consensus on literacy instruction that will allow the principal to assess the quality of literacy instruction in an effective manner? There are five rules that can be useful to keep the committee work productive and manageable (see Table 6.1).

The committee will also want to do some research of its own. A first step might be to embark upon an examination of best, research-based literacy instructional practices. This will ensure that everyone is on the same page regarding what good literacy instruction should look like in the classroom. A second step could be to review the district-level evaluation processes as they relate specifically to literacy instruction. This will help to avoid duplicating what is already in place while pointing the committee toward areas of the evaluation tool that may not relate to literacy instruction. Finally, the committee might consider developing performance indicators and "look fors."

With all of this information, the committee can begin to formulate their ideas and draft the supplemental evaluation system. Once the committee has formulated some of their ideas, they should be reviewed by teachers who were not a part of the committee. Perhaps someone from the district office or another building-level administrator could also offer suggestions.

TABLE 6.1. Rules for Productive Committee Work

Rule	Rationale
1. The focus of the work must be on student achievement.	It is important for committee members to agree that the goal is not to determine who should stay or leave but how the school can ensure that students are getting the appropriate instruction that is needed for academic success, especially in the area of literacy achievement.
2. Group decisions will be reached through consensus.	When members cannot support a particular recommendation, ask the person to provide suggestions for changing the recommendation that will gain their support.
3. No decisions are reached on a topic until it has been considered by the committee at least twice.	Consider starting each meeting with an opportunity to review the work from the prior meeting. This practice will allow committee members the time to engage in reflective committee work. By doing so, committee members will not feel rushed to make a decision. Remember, it is for the benefit of the students, not an exercise in futility. You want to engage in a process that will yield a tool that will add value to the district's current evaluation system.
4. The committee should have a clear focus.	At the beginning of the committee's work, it is important that it is understood that the process is not to change your literacy program but to effectively measure the success of the literacy efforts in your building, thus leading to continuous literacy improvement.
5. Assign a co-facilitator for the committee.	An important aspect of this role will be the development of meaningful agendas that will help facilitate the work. Facilitators should function as discussion leaders. The facilitators must ensure that each member of the committee has an opportunity to share ideas and opinions. Facilitators should look for emerging themes, concerns, and agreements.

Once the supplemental system has been used in the evaluation process, the committee should be reconvened to determine if the desired results were achieved and whether the vision and mission were met. Adjustments may need to be made. Remember, this tool is for you and your building; it does not have to look like anyone else's.

The Use of Performance Indicators and "Look Fors"

As mentioned earlier in this chapter, the building committee should consider a process that will supplement the district model. One way to do this effectively is by developing performance indicators and "look fors," as defined by Stronge and

Tucker (2005). These performance indicators and instructional look fors can be used by the building administrator to gauge the effectiveness of the literacy program. Again, it is important to remember that the goal for the committee is not to create an evaluation system; rather the goal is to supplement the district's evaluation tools in order to have a better understanding of how literacy is being taught in the school.

Identifying specific *performance indicators* that align with each person's identified responsibility can be a useful process. The following example demonstrates how one job responsibility can be assessed differently depending upon the performance indicators that are identified. In this example, a job responsibility for both the literacy coach/specialist and Reading Recovery teachers read, "Consults/collaborates with school personnel." While the responsibility is identical, the performance indicators are not, and they allow the principal to differentiate these very different positions during the evaluation process. The indicators for the literacy specialist/coach included the following:

- Meets with individual teachers and teams to assist in planning instructional units that reflect district curriculum standards and objectives
- Assists teachers to incorporate reading and writing strategies in other subjects
- Works cooperatively with learning and enrichment resource specialists and guidance counselors to ensure that the needs of students are met
- Works with the curriculum leaders, teachers, and other staff members to facilitate curriculum integration

On the other hand, the indicators for the Reading Recovery teachers were different, because they were aligned with these teachers' primary role in the school. The performance indicators for "Consults/collaborates with school personnel" included the following:

- Meets regularly with individual teachers and teams
- Shares assessment data with teachers
- Participates in parent conferences with teachers
- Observes students in regular classrooms as needed
- Provides literacy intervention for students based on the prescribed model

For many positions within a school, there are responsibilities that will have similar performance indicators. The performance indicators, however, are one way that an evaluation system can be supplemented to ensure that the principal is looking for specific behaviors that make a difference in the literacy environment.

It is important to recognize that performance indicators are not all-inclusive but are intended to provide a guide for the process. Once the committee identifies the performance indicators for various responsibilities, the committee can develop an assessment rubric that can serve as a guide for principals. Figure 6.2 provides one example of performance indicators for the literacy specialist/coach and Reading Recovery teacher in a school district and the agreed-upon rubric used to guide administrators.

Another way to supplement a district tool is to develop observation tools that reflect the literacy practices wanted in the school. Look fors are a resource that principals can use to guide their observation of literacy classroom practices. While they are not designed to be evaluative in nature, they can provide useful information about literacy practices in the school. For example, the primary-grade classroom might have look fors that indicate whether teachers provide a variety of opportunities for students as well as look fors about the physical environment:

- Teacher is providing opportunities for reading . . .

    To children
    With children
    By children
    One-on-one reading
    Read-alouds
    Whole group

- Teacher provides for students . . .

    Word walls
    Reading labels in the classroom
    Student class name charts and/or cards

Look fors can be general or specific. The Maya Angelou Elementary School in Pasco, Washington, for example, has on their website a list of look fors that help visitors understand their belief system. Included in this list are look fors in the classroom, with students and with teachers. Looks fors at Maya Angelou include:

Classroom

Students organized in groups
Variety of reading materials
Word walls
Print-rich environment
Literature circles

Intervention/Instruction for the Reading Specialist

I-1. Demonstrates current, accurate, and comprehensive knowledge consistent with the profession
- Exhibits an understanding of the reading process
- Uses professional literature and current resources
- Models strategies grounded in current research of reading
- Understands the multiple causes of reading difficulties

I-2. Creates an organized and positive learning environment
- Maintains an organized and accessible resource room
- Maintains instructional materials
- Provides books and materials in sufficient quantity (within budget constraints)

I-5. Provides direct services/instruction on a short-term basis
- Works with students to determine strengths and needs
- Plans and implements instruction based on identified strengths and needs
- Models reading strategies which promote individual student engagement
- Seeks feedback from classroom teacher regarding the effectiveness of the instruction

Intervention/Instruction for Reading Recovery

I-1. Demonstrates current, accurate, and comprehensive knowledge consistent with the profession
- Exhibits an understanding of the reading process
- Uses professional literature and current resources
- Models strategies grounded in current research of reading

I-2. Creates an organized and positive learning environment
- Demonstrates understanding of the influence of the physical setting, schedule, routines, and transitions on students
- Uses schedule, routines, and transitions to promote learning
- Maintains instructional materials/equipment in good repair
- Provides materials and equipment in sufficient quantity

I-5. Provides direct services/instruction which promotes student learning
- Works with students to determine strengths and needs
- Plans and implements Reading Recovery instruction
- Uses questions appropriate to Reading Recovery lesson
- Seeks feedback from classroom teacher regarding the effectiveness of the instruction

FIGURE 6.2. Sample responsibilities and performance indicators for reading personnel, from *Williamsburg–James City County Public Schools.*

Students

Reading self-selected materials

Buddy reading

Responding orally and in writing

Holding literature discussions

Asking each other questions

Teachers

Motivate students to read

Use modeling

Engage in think-alouds

Read aloud to students

Conference with students

Newport News Schools in Virginia use look fors to provide more specific instructional strategies that you might expect to see used during classroom instruction. Figure 6.3 provides sample look fors in literacy instruction used in this district. The sample is not intended to be comprehensive.

WHAT KIND OF DATA SHOULD BE COLLECTED?

As principals attempt to determine how effective literacy instruction is in their schools, they need to consider a variety of data sources to ensure that they have the most comprehensive picture possible of their staff members and the success of their literacy program. In addition to looking at student assessment data, principals should consider other means of determining performance: walk-throughs, data talks, client surveys, self-evaluations, peer evaluations, and portfolios. One method of gathering data simply will not provide a complete picture of student achievement or measure teacher success in delivery.

Student Assessments

Given the many hats that building-level administrators wear on a daily basis, it is important to have a consistent approach to monitoring the success of the school's instructional program and, in particular, the literacy program. Monitoring student achievement is a first step. Student achievement, however, can be determined with a variety of data, as discussed in Chapter 4. Essential questions to consider include the following:

Lesson component	Elementary
Engage and hook	Enduring understanding Essential questions What students should know and be able to do Prior knowledge
Explain and model	**Reading—What:** Phonemic awareness Phonics Vocabulary Focus skill Focus strategy **Writing—How:** Think-alouds Read-alouds Graphic organizers Leveled texts **Writing—What:** Composing Written expression Usage/mechanics **Writing—How:** Modeled writing Shared writing Guided writing Interactive writing
Explore and apply	Guided practice Independent practice Collaborative groups Student-centered tasks
Evaluate	Projects Tests/quizzes Observations Retelling

FIGURE 6.3. Sample lesson "look fors." Sample reading instructional delivery components for reading personnel, Newport News Public Schools. Reprinted by permission.

- What data will be needed to effectively gauge student success?
- How often will the data be collected?
- Who will be responsible for the data collection?
- How will the data by analyzed and by whom?
- How will the results be used?

Data collected from state-mandated, districtwide, and schoolwide assessments must be disaggregated for individual students and considered in conjunction with other data (e.g., student portfolio, work samples, grades, etc.). The data collection processes must occur regularly, be as simple as possible, and be deliberate and purposeful. Student assessment data is an important source of information when evaluating staff members, but it is only one source.

Also, keep in mind the three guiding questions mentioned earlier in this chapter that the committee should have addressed: (Why are we evaluating? What are we evaluating? How are we evaluating?). The answers to those questions will guide the amount and kind of data collected.

While we have all heard the clich? a thousand times, "What gets monitored is what gets done," it still prevails. Attention to the type of assessments that are being used to generate information about staff members is an integral part of any system. In other words, do the assessment instruments that are being used at the school adequately and effectively measure the quality of literacy instruction? Additionally, it is important to remember that the frequency with which students are assessed is worthy of consideration and discussion. Much of this has already been discussed in Chapter 4.

The Walk-through

A walk-through is exactly what it sounds like—the principal walks through the building and informally observes classroom instruction. Also known as "management by walking around" (MBWA), it allows the principal to informally, and in many cases unexpectedly, observe both the students and teacher in action. On the website *www.futurecents.com/mainmbwa.htm*, 12 guidelines for MBWA are outlined that generally speak to corporate management (Future Cents, 2008). Here, the guidelines have been adapted to address MBWA from an educational perspective while leaving the integrity of their purpose in tact.

1. *Do it to everyone.* Visit the classroom of all teachers, not just literacy teachers.
2. *Do it as often as you can.* Be visible often; this demonstrates your interest in the teachers' work and students' progress.
3. *Go by yourself.* This will encourage honest dialogue from teachers and students.

4. *Do not circumvent subordinate managers.* If teachers (or students) are apt to discuss confidential matters or offer complaints about colleagues, remind them of proper protocol for such concerns.
5. *Ask questions.* Observe student–teacher interactions. Ask about the lesson that is being taught, ongoing projects, objectives and goals for the lesson, and so on. Be careful not to appear to be intrusive.
6. *Watch and listen.* Listen for the words and tone of the teacher and the students. This can help to determine motivation levels and whether the students understand the lesson.
7. *Share your dreams with them.* Share your vision.
8. *Try out their work.* Take the opportunity to teach a lesson or class. Substitute for a teacher who may need to leave early, or teach the class with the teacher present. This will give you the opportunity to gain the teacher's perspective. (This guideline may take longer than just a few minutes, but the information gained can be valuable.)
9. *Bring good news.* Share information on recent successes. Check student grades ahead of time and discuss their success or ways they can be more successful. Share with the teacher noted successes among his or her students. Here is a example of bringing good news to a classroom:

   > "Good morning, Ms. Jones. I would just like to share with you and your class that everyone in this class passed the reading statewide assessment. Congratulations and keep up the good work."

10. *Have fun.* This is an opportunity to show that, while school requires work on everyone's part, learning can be fun. Demonstrate your lighter side without being clownish.
11. *Catch them in the act of doing something good.* Offer "Caught Doing Good" awards. Randomly select a teacher or student who is doing outstanding work or has demonstrated marked improvement and give them an award or prize. You could provide lunch for a student or cover a class for the teacher allowing him/her an extra free period for a day.
12. *Do not be critical.* If you witness a lesson "gone wrong," do not openly criticize the teacher (or student). Privately ask for clarifying information and provide guidance on how things could be done differently (*www.futurecents.com/mainmbwa.htm*).

Downey, Steffy, English, Frase, and Poston (2004) note that the primary purpose of the walk-through is to promote dialogue about instruction between the principal and teacher. There are generally three elements of a walk-through: (1) they are brief, (2) they are focused, and (3) they are followed by some type of conversation about the visit. The brevity of the visits (around three minutes in each classroom) allows the principal to get snapshots of their teachers at work. Over a period of time, these snapshots can reveal a pattern within a classroom or across the school.

Prior to or just after a walk-through, principals may also ask focus questions that relate to a schoolwide goal. For example, if there is a goal related to improved reading comprehension, a principal might share this question with the teachers: How do you ensure that your students are actively reading for meaning during their lessons with you? This type of focus question can be shared at the beginning of the week, so that teachers know that during the walk-through, the principal will be looking for active comprehension strategies. Other times, principals might ask individual teachers to reflect on questions tied directly to their personal classroom practices or goals.

Walk-throughs can provide endless examples of literacy in action. A principal, for example, might want to focus on writing practices. In this case, the principal would look for evidence that:

- Students are actively involved in writing.
- Student writing is displayed on classroom walls.
- Students use journals.
- Students can explain the writing process
- Prompts for journal writing are displayed.

Principals have noted a lot of benefits to walk-throughs. First, walk-throughs get principals into classrooms much more frequently, which enhances their understanding of what teachers are doing and how they approach literacy instruction on a daily or weekly basis. An unexpected benefit of walk-throughs is that teachers see their principals as much more invested in classroom instruction. Being in the classroom on a regular basis allows teachers to see principals as active members of the learning community. Walk-throughs are also a good basis for sharing effective practices with individual staff and with a faculty as a whole. Some principals even share what they have seen at staff meetings and encourage their staff members to share their practices.

As the building-level administrator, it is critical to keep in mind the purpose of a walk-through. The walk-through is an opportunity to get a snapshot of literacy instruction in the building at a given moment; neither the administrator nor the teacher should view it as a "dog and pony show." Rather, it is an opportunity to see the delivery of literacy instruction and student engagement at the purest level. In order to ensure that walk-throughs are meaningful, identify the look fors at the beginning of each week. Without a focus, administrators may fall into the trap of trying to observe every aspect of the lesson versus specific segments that contribute to a good literacy lesson. Making walk-throughs a daily or weekly practice will add value to the evaluation process. Figure 6.4 presents a sample observation form that can guide the look fors during a walk-through. These observation forms are easy to develop and can really focus the observation.

Teacher ______________________ School ______________________

Date __________ Time __________ Observer ______________________

Reading:

Comprehension strategies

- ☐ Prior knowledge accessed
- ☐ Guided reading
  - ☐ whole group
  - ☐ small group
- ☐ Independent reading
- ☐ Paired reading
- ☐ Picture reading
- ☐ Mental images created by teacher
- ☐ Assessment
  - ☐ formal
  - ☐ informal

Writing:

Process

- ☐ Writing activities
  - ☐ Prompts
  - ☐ Independent
  - ☐ Conferencing
- ☐ Word wall
- ☐ Interactive writing
- ☐ Student-made dictionary
- ☐ Connections
  - ☐ to current lesson
  - ☐ child's experience
  - ☐ other ______________________
- ☐ Assessment
  - ☐ formal
  - ☐ informal

Comments:

FIGURE 6.4. Sample walk-through observation form..

Some principals have also developed forms that identify expectations for how the literacy blocks of time should be used. They have then used these forms to guide their walk-through. The advantage of these forms is that they provide teachers, especially beginning teachers, with a road map of how their day and week should proceed. Figure 6.5 provides an example of expected elementary literacy practices for a school.

Data Talks

Another consideration for evaluating staff is the use of data talks. Data talks serve as an opportunity to meet with the staff to discuss the data that have been gathered through walk-throughs, observations, student assessments, teachers' observations

Week:

Grade	Focus Skill and Strategies
Kindergarten	
First	
Second	
Third	
Fourth	
Fifth	

Day 1	Day 2	Day 3	Day 4 and Additional Days
30–40 Minutes Whole Group: • Building background, genre, essential questions • Explain and model focus skill/ strategy • Model with big book, related read-aloud / sharing literature selection, content text, genre or author study • Vocabulary • Phonemic awareness work K/1 • Phonics work K–2 **50–60 Minutes Small Groups:** (2–3 groups) Skills-focused lesson or guided reading—use Harcourt Leveled Readers, Intervention Reader, or supplemental text	**30–50 Minutes Whole Group:** • Building background, genre • Vocabulary work • Model using anthology selection/ shared reading (Longer anthology selections may be finished on the next day) • Phonemic awareness work K/1, phonics work K–2 as needed **50–60 Minutes Small Groups:** (Approx 3 groups) Skills-focused lesson or guided reading—complete Harcourt Leveled Readers, Intervention Reader, supplemental text	**20–30 Minutes Whole Group:** • Model with completion of anthology story if needed or select text for read-aloud/ shared reading: Harcourt companion text or sharing literature selection, content text, genre or author study, related text • Vocabulary work as needed • Phonemic awareness work K/1, phonics work K–2 as needed **60–70 Minutes Small Groups:** Approx. 3) Skills-focused lesson or guided reading—leveled text	**20–30 Minutes Whole Group:** • Select text for read-aloud/ shared reading: content text, genre or author study, related text • Vocabulary work as needed • Phonemic awareness work K/1, phonics work K–2 as needed **60–70 Minutes Small Groups:** (Approx. 3) Skills-focused lesson or guided reading- leveled text

FIGURE 6.5. Elementary reading expected practices. Sample reading blocks schedule for reading instruction, Newport News Public Schools. Reprinted by permission.

of student progress, portfolios, and any other means. Data talk sessions should yield information regarding students who are reading on, below, or above grade level, strategies that are used for struggling students, and accomplishments as well as challenges.

These sessions can also be used to devise intervention plans or next steps to help students who continue to struggle in literacy and to evaluate whether current plans and interventions are appropriate. The following is a list of sample questions that can be provided to the staff before the data talk session begins. Principals should, however, devise their own list of questions that are specific to their building program.

- How are you using the district reading curriculum?
- What assessments tools did you use to assess students' reading comprehension?
- What instructional strategies have been most useful? How do you know they are successful?
- Which readers are struggling? How do you know?
- What trends do you see for your class (or grade level)?
- What conclusions did you draw from these trends?
- What are the next steps for your struggling students?
- What strategies will you include?
- Why did you choose these strategies?
- How will you know that these strategies made a difference?

One way to accomplish the goal of creating meaningful data talks is to establish the expectation that grade-level team meetings will incorporate reading data talks into their meetings. During the talks, the principal can use the data talk questions (mentioned earlier) as a springboard to gain more insight into how teachers are using students' reading data to make instructional decisions.

Client Surveys

Client surveys represent another source of information about staff (and ourselves) and can be used to gather input from students, parents, and teachers. Surveys can be used to provide feedback to teachers for their professional growth. They can also be shared with administrators, although teachers may not be comfortable with this at first. Some systems require teachers to note the date surveys were administered within their portfolio, along with a reflective comment, but do not require sharing them with their supervisors.

Student Surveys

Students in elementary schools are not often asked for feedback by their teachers, but this feedback can be useful. Survey items for students may vary depending upon their grade level. Primary-age children, for example, can be asked to respond to statements such as "My teacher helps me when I need it" or "My teacher shows us how to do new things" with a simple yes or no. Upper-elementary students, on the other hand, may respond to items such as "The teacher generally gives me work that makes me think" or "The teacher encourages me to ask and answer questions in class" by writing a comment explaining their answer. Student surveys can be given yearly or every other year, depending on the needs identified by the committee. In one district, nontenured teachers were required to administer these more frequently than tenured teachers.

Parent Surveys

Parent surveys also provide useful information, and many times the information is more positive than teachers expect. The parent surveys that are most useful are those that tap into what parents know firsthand. Items such as "The teacher communicates in an understandable way" or "The teacher sets high expectations and helps my child to reach them" are examples of these. Surveys do not have to be distributed every year but should be distributed frequently enough to help the teacher identify any issues that may be emerging.

Teacher Surveys

Teacher surveys are useful for those literacy coaches or specialists (and other building personnel) who work primarily in a collaborative manner with other teachers. Teacher surveys can use a scaled rating (strongly agree to strongly disagree) and can provide these coaches and specialists with useful information. Items such as "Communicates effectively with me regarding student progress and school programs" or "Makes me feel comfortable about asking for help" can provide valuable feedback to the consulting coach or specialist.

More districts and schools are using surveys as one way to get additional viewpoints on how the school staff members are doing.

Self-Evaluations

Self-evaluation can occur in a variety of ways, including through journals, through videos, through conversations with peers, and through portfolios (which will be discussed later in this chapter). When teachers use journals as a mechanism for self-reflection, they are often reflecting on day-to-day classroom instruction. In this process, they may try to reconstruct the classroom lesson and analyze each variable that affected the quality of this lesson. Bullard (1998) suggests that teachers "stop in the teaching process, think about their work, and make sense of it" (p. 000). This type of self-reflection may also incorporate dialogue with colleagues about best practices in the classroom.

When teachers use portfolios for self-evaluation, they typically gather tangible evidence (documentation) of their classroom instruction. This evidence provides a structured way to document teaching practices and reflect on the way in which a teacher provides instruction. Portfolio content will vary based upon what is being taught and measured; however, there may be some standard items that could be included in the portfolio, such as representative lesson plans, student work samples, and reflective commentary. Documentation of self-reflection can be kept in a journal, as stated earlier, or in a portfolio that is shared with the principal as a part of the overall evaluation process. When shared with the principal, the principal assumes the role of active listener and supporter to guide the teacher toward continuous improvement in classroom instruction.

Peer Evaluations

Peer evaluations are not a new concept, but are often used in higher education rather than K–12 education. A peer evaluation program does not supplant principal evaluations; rather it serves as a complement to it and is designed to improve teaching. Peer evaluators observe classroom instruction, assist with lesson planning, provide feedback, and may even model teaching a lesson.

A program that was developed in Cincinnati public schools allows experienced teachers to leave their classroom for 2 years to serve as mentors or peer evaluators. The 2-year cycles are set up in an effort to keep mentors or peer evaluators in touch with being a classroom instructor. The evaluation program is not just for beginning teachers but also for veteran teachers who require intervention. In Cincinnati, it was determined that teachers would rather be evaluated by someone who knows their particular subject area and who is in touch with the realities of the classroom. The program is controversial, because the peer evaluators also have the authority to determine whether teacher contracts will be renewed (Miner, 1992). Certainly, it is not the norm that peer evaluators have the authority to determine continued employment for teachers.

The success of any peer evaluation lies in the willingness of both teachers (evaluator and evaluatee) to participate in the process. As with principal–teacher observations and evaluations, there should be a preconference to discuss materials, the goals and objectives for the lesson(s), and teacher and student expectations. A postconference should always take place to discuss what was observed, with strengths and weaknesses noted.

The peer evaluator must be prepared to work with the teacher and help seek out resources to build up areas weakness. In these cases, the burden on the peer evaluator is tremendous, because they must be honest and willing to provide constructive feedback in a respectful manner to a colleague.

Portfolios

Portfolios provide an opportunity for teachers to participate in data collection by maintaining their own collection of materials. Tucker, Gareis, Stronge, and Beers (2000) present evidence that portfolios can provide documentation that teachers are meeting their teaching responsibilities and that teachers do select meaningful documents to demonstrate their work. Their research also concluded that principals were able to provide greater differentiation among teachers when they used a portfolio than when they did not, with the ability to better discriminate between capable teachers and truly exceptional ones. We believe that this finding is due to the fact that the portfolio provides the building principal with more information than is typically available to them.

Sample activities that can be included in the portfolio might include the following:

- A lesson/intervention plan
- Written evidence of integrating writing and reading into classroom instruction
- An annotated list of instructional activities for a unit
- Annotated samples of photographs of instructional materials written or created by the teacher
- A brief report describing the record-keeping system
- A copy of a scoring rubric used for a student project or report
- A log of inservice/staff development activities with a brief description of each
- Copies of materials submitted to professional newsletters or journals
- Evidence of professional presentations
- Sample student surveys

A number of schools have found that the portfolio is an important piece of the monitoring fabric. If a principal decides to incorporate teacher portfolios, it is important to provide teachers with guidelines. Guidelines will help to ensure that teachers will collect artifacts that will enable the principal to determine the teacher's progress toward addressing the students' literacy needs. What should be avoided at all costs is the "catch-all folder." The following considerations are important before implementing a portfolio system:

- Purpose—What will be accomplished?
- Procedures—What will be the implications for teaching and learning?
- Contents—What will be included?

- Audience—Who will benefit from the information?
- Reviewers—Who will have access and for what purpose?
- Parental Involvement—Will parents/guardians be involved?
- Timelines—How often will the portfolio be collected?

The use of portfolios has gained support over the years, and the effective use of portfolios is an excellent tool to determine teacher progress. However, to suggest that everyone in your building will be enthusiastic about the time required would be misleading. On the other hand, when used appropriately, portfolios will enhance the evaluation process. As stated earlier, the portfolio helps to overcome what is often viewed as a "one-size-fits-all" teacher evaluation system that limits the administrator's ability to recognize varied teaching responsibilities. When used for its intended purpose, a portfolio will allow an administrator to see progress over time and to determine areas of needed growth for the teacher.

RESOURCES

There are several resources available to assist principals when assessing teachers' reading instruction. Two sources that can aid principals are: *Teaching Reading* (Honig, Diamond, & Gutlohn, 2000) and *The Principal's Guide to Raising Reading Achievement* (McEwan, 1998). An excellent resource for information on implementing student portfolios in the classroom is *The Portfolio Book: A Step-by-Step Guide for Teachers* (Shores & Grace, 1998).

Honig, B., Diamond, L., & Gutlohn, L. (2000). *Teaching reading.* Novato, CA: Arena Press.

McEwan, E. K. (1998). The *principal's guide to raising reading achievement.* Thousand Oaks, CA: Corwin Press.

Shores, E. F., & Grace, C. (1998). *The portfolio book: A step-by-step guide for teachers. Beltsville, MD:* Gryphon House.

CONCLUSIONS

Evaluating teachers is critical yet often uncomfortable. This chapter has discussed the national context for teacher evaluation and the research regarding best practices in teacher evaluation. In addition to the district's evaluation plan, principals should consider developing a plan to supplement the evaluation system so that a more comprehensive picture of the teacher emerges. The use of portfolios, walk-throughs, data talks, client surveys, self-evaluations, and peer evaluations was presented and discussed.

REFERENCES

Abouzeid, M. (2006, June 15). *The role of professional development in reading instruction: The Virginia model.* Presentation to the Webconference, Norfolk State University, Norfolk, VA.

Acheson, K., & Gall, M. (1997). *Techniques in the clinical supervision of teachers.* New York: Longman.

Adams, M. (1990). *Beginning to read.* Cambridge, MA: Harvard University Press.

Adler, M. (1982). *The Padeia proposal: An educational manifesto.* New York: Macmillan.

Afflerbach, P. (2007). *Understanding and using reading assessment.* Newark, DE: International Reading Association.

Almasi, J. F. (1995). The nature of fourth graders' sociocognitive conflicts in peer-led and teacher-led discussions of literature. *Reading Research Quarterly, 30*, 314–351.

Alvermann, D. (1991). The discussion web: A graphic aid for learning across the curriculum. *The Reading Teacher, 45*(2), 92–99.

Banks, J. (1999). *An introduction to multicultural education* (2nd ed.). Boston: Allyn & Bacon.

Baumann, J., & Kame'enui, E. (Eds.), (2004). *Vocabulary instruction: Research to practice.* New York: Guilford Press.

Bear, D., Invernizzi, Templeton, S., & Johnston, F. (2008). *Words their way: Word study for phonics, vocabulary, and spelling instruction* (4th ed.). Upper Saddle River, NJ: Pearson Education.

Beck, I. L., McKeown, M. G., & Kucan, L. (2002). *Bringing words to life: Robust vocabulary instruction.* New York: Guilford Press.

Berg, A., Melaville, A., & Blank, M. J. (2007). *Community and family engagement: Principals share what works.* Alexandria, VA: Coalition for Community Schools.

Best Practices Brief. (December 2004). School climate and learning in Michigan State University. No. 31.

Blachowicz, C., & Fisher, P. (2006). *Teaching vocabulary in all classrooms.* New York: Prentice Hall.

Blachowicz, C., & Ogle, D. (2008). *Reading comprehension: Strategies for independent learners.* New York: Guilford Press.

Brown, R. (2008). The road not yet taken: A transactional strategies approach to comprehension instruction. *The Reading Teacher, 61*(7), 538–547.

Bullard, B. (1998). *Teacher self-evaluation.* Paper presented at the annual meeting of the Mid-South Educational Research Association, New Orleans, LA.

California State Board of Education (1998). English-language arts content standards for California public schools, kindergarten through grade twelve. Sacramento, CA: California Department of Education.

Canady, R., & Rettig, M. (1995). The power of innovative scheduling. *Educational Leadership, 53*(3), 4–10.

Cassell, R. N. (1999). The American academy of school psychology offers promise for school problems and "a nation at risk." *Education, 119*, 584–587.

Chall, J. (1983). *Stages of reading development.* New York: McGraw-Hill.

Cobb, C. (2005). Literacy teams: Sharing leadership to improve student learning. *The Reading Teacher, 58*(5), 472–474.

Cohen, D. (1995). *What standards for national standards? Phi Delta Kappan, 76*, 740–741.

Colby, S. Bradshaw, L., & Joyner, R. (2002). *Teacher evaluation: A review of the literature.* Paper presented at the Annual Meeting of AERA, New Orleans, LA.

Cook, C. J., & Fine, C. (1997a). *Critical issue: Finding time for professional development.* Available at *www.ncrel.org/sdrs/areas/issues/educatrs/profdevl/pd300.htm.*

Cook, C. J., & Fine, C. S. (1997b). *Critical issue: Evaluating professional growth and development.* Available at *http://www.ncrel.org/sdrs/areas/issues/educatrs/profdevl/pd500.htm.*

Cooper, J. D. (2003). *Literacy: Helping children construct meaning* (5th ed.). Boston: Houghton Mifflin.

Cooper, J. D., & Kiger, N. (2005). *Literacy assessment: Helping teachers plan instruction.* Boston: Houghton Mifflin.

Cooper, J., & Pikulski, J. (2000). *A research-based framework for Houghton Mifflin Reading: A legacy of literacy.* Boston: Houghton Mifflin.

Corcoran, T. B. (1995). *Helping teachers teach well: Transforming professional development* (CPRE Policy Briefs). Consortium for Policy Research in Education.

Culham, R. (2003). *6 + 1 traits of writing: The complete guide.* New York: Scholastic.

Cunningham, P. (2005). Phonics they use: Words for reading and writing. (4th Ed.) Boston: Pearson/Allyn & Bacon.

Cunningham, P., Hall, D., & DeFee, M. (1998). Non-ability grouped, multi-leveled instruction: Eight years later. *The Reading Teacher, 51*, 652–664.

Dansereau, D. (1986). *Dyadic and cooperative learning and performance strategies.* Paper presented at the annual meeting of American Educational Research Association, San Francisco, CA.

Darling-Hammond, L. (1997). *Doing what matters most: Investing in quality teaching.* New York: National Commission on Teaching and America's Future.

Deal, T., & Kennedy, A. (2000). Corporate Cultures. New York, NY: Perseus Books Publishing, LLC.

Deal, T., & Peterson, K. (2002). *Shaping school culture field book.* San Francisco: Jossey-Bass.

Deal, T., & Peterson, K. (2003). *Shaping school culture: The heart of leadership.* San Francisco: Jossey-Bass.

Delaney, M., Toburen, L., Hooten, B., & Dozier, A. (1997). Parallel block scheduling spells success. *Educational Leadership, 55*(4), 61–63.

DeLisio, E. (2009). Planning for parent involvement. Education World. Available at www.education-world.com/a.admin/admin/admin421.shtml.

Downey, C., Steffy, B., English, F., Frase, L., & Poston, W. (2004). *The three-minute classroom walk-through: Changing school supervisor practices one teacher at a time.* Thousand Oaks, CA: Corwin Press.

DuFour, R., & Berkey, T. (1995). The principal as staff developer. *Journal of Staff Development, 16*(9). Available at *www.nsdc.org/library/publications/jsd/jsddufour.cfm.*

DuFour, R., & Eaker, R. (1998). *Professional learning communities at work: Best practices for enhancing student achievement.* Bloomington, IN: National Education Service.

DuPree, M. (1989). *Leadership is an art.* New York: Dell.

Duttweiler, P. C. (2000). *Do we practice what we preach?* Clemson, SC: National Dropout Prevention Center.

Educational Testing Service. (2003). *Early literacy assessment systems: Essential elements.* Princeton, NJ: Author.

Ehri, L. (1995). Phases of learning to read words by sight. *Journal of Research in Reading, 18,* 116–125.

Fielding, L., Kerr, N., & Rosier, P. (2007). *Annual growth for all students, Catch-up growth for those who are behind.* Kennewick, WA: New Foundation Press.

Fountas, I. C., & Pinnell, G. S. (1996). *Guided reading: Good first teaching for all children.* Portsmouth, NH: Heinemann.

Friedman, T. (2005). *The world is flat: A brief history of the twenty-first century.* New York: Farrar, Straus & Giroux.

Fullan, M. (1995), *Change forces: Probing the depths of educational reform.* London: Falmer Press.

Fullan, M., & Miles, M. (1992). Getting reform right: What works and what doesn't. *Phi Delta Kappan, 73*(10), 744–752.

FutureCents website; *www.futurecents.com/mainmbwa.htm.* Retrieved on April 23, 2008.

FutureCents. Management by walking around. Retrieved May 6, 2008, from *www.futurecents.com/mainmbwa.htm.*

Gaffney, J. S., Hesbol, K., & Corso, L. (2005). *Is your school fit for literacy? 10 areas of action for principals.* Naperville, IL: Learning Point Associates.

Gambrell, L., & Almasi, J. (Eds.) (1996). *Lively discussions! Fostering engaged reading.* Newark, DE: International Reading Association.

Ganske, K. (2006). *Word sorts and more: Sound, pattern, and meaning explorations, K–3.* New York: Guilford Press.

Gaskins, I. (2005). *Success with struggling readers: The Benchmark School approach.* New York: Guilford Press.

Goodlad, J. (1984). *A place called school.* New York: McGraw Hill.

Grady, E. (1992). *The portfolio assessment approach to assessment* (Fastback 341). Bloomington, IN: Phi Delta Kappa Educational Foundation.

Haggard, M. (1986). The vocabulary self-selection strategy: Using student interest and word knowledge to enhance vocabulary growth. *Journal of Reading, 29,* 634–642.

Hall, G., & Horde, S. (2001). Implementing change: Patterns, principles, and potholes. Needham Heights, MA: Allyn and Bacon.

Hammond, A., & Reynolds, L. (1999). *Developing Literacy Partnerships.* South Melbourne, Australia: Addison Wesley Longman.

Hart, B., & Risley, T. R. (2003). *The early catastrophe: The 30 million word gap by age 3.* Retrieved January 10, 2009, from *www.aft.org/pubs-reports/american_educator/spring2003/catastrophe.html.*

Haynes, M. (2007). *From state policy to classroom practice: Improving literacy instruction for all students.* Washington, DC: National Association of School Boards of Education.

Hoover-Dempsey, K. V., & Sandler, H. M. (1997). Why do parents become involved in their children's education? *Review of Educational Research, 67,* 3–42.

International Reading Association and National Association for the Education of Young Children National Council of Teachers of English. (1996). *Standards for the English language arts*. Urbana, IL/Newark, DE: Author. Available at *www.ncte.org/about/over/standards/110846.htm*.

International Reading Association and National Association for the Education of Young Children (1998). Learning to read and write: Developmentally appropriate practices for young children. *Young Children, 53*(4): 30–46.

International Reading Association. (2002). *Family–school partnerships*. Newark, DE: Author.

International Reading Association. (2004). *The role and qualifications of the reading coach in the United States*. Newark, DE: International Reading Association.

Johns, J. (2005). *Basic reading inventory* (9th ed.). Dubuque, IA: Kendall/Hunt.

Johnson, J. (2002). Staying ahead of the game. *Educational Leadership, 59,* 26–30.

Johnston, P. (1987). Teachers as evaluation experts. *The Reading Teacher, 40,* 744–748.

Joint Committee on Standards for Educational Evaluation (2007). *The Personnel Evaluation Standards*. Newbury Park, CA: Corwin Press.

Joyce, B., & Showers, B. (1996). Staff development as a comprehensive service organization. *Journal of Staff Development, 17*(1), 2–6.

Learning First Alliance. (2000). *Every child reading: A professional development guide*. Baltimore: Association for Supervision and Curriculum Development.

Lenski, S., Ehlers-Zavala, F., Daniel, M., & Sun-Irminger, X. (2006). Assessing English-language learners in mainstream classrooms. *The Reading Teacher, 60,* 24–34.

McDiarmid, G. W. (1995). *Realizing new learning for all students: A framework for the professional development of Kentucky teachers*. East Lansing, MI: National Center for Research on Teacher Learning.

Marzano, R. (2003). What works in Schools: Translating research into action. Alexandria, VA: Association for Supervision and Curriculum Development.

McLaughlin, M. W. (1991). Test-based accountability as a reform strategy. *Phi Delta Kappan 73*(3), 248–251.

Miner, B. (1992). Teachers evaluating teachers. *Rethinking Schools*. Retrieved May 6, 2008, from *www.rethinkingschools.org/special_reports/union/uneval.shtml*.

Moore, D. W., Moore, S. A., Cunningham, P. M., & Cunningham, J. (2003). *Developing readers and writers in the content areas k-12*. Boston: Allyn & Bacon.

Morrow, L., & Smith, J. (1990). The effects of group size on interactive storybook reading. *Reading Research Quarterly, 25,* 213–231.

Moskal, M. K., & Blachowicz, C. (2006). *Partnering for fluency*. New York: Guilford Press.

Nagy, W. (1988). *Teaching vocabulary to improve comprehension*. Urbana, IL/Newark, DE: National Council of Teachers of English and International Reading Association.

National Association of State Boards of Education. (2000, February). *Teacher Evaluation, 8,* 1.

National Center for Education Statistics. (2003). The nation's report card: Reading 2002. Washington, DC: National Center for Education Statistics.

National Center for Public Policy & Higher Education: Policy Alert, November 2005.

National Central Regional Educational Laboratory, (2004). Critical Issue: Monitoring the school literacy program. Retrieved May 5, 1008 from *www.ncrel.org/sdrs/areas/issues/content/cntareas/reading/li700.htm*.

National Council for Teachers of English and the International Reading Association. (1996). Standards for the English language arts. Urbana, IL/Newark, E: Author. Available at *www.ncte.org/about/over/standards/1108/6.html*.

National Reading Panel. (2000). *Teaching children to read: An evidence-based assessment of the scientific research literature on reading and its implications for reading instruction.* Washington, DC: National Institute of Child Health and Human Development.

National Research Council. (1998). *Starting out right.* Washington, DC: National Academy Press.

National School Boards Association. (2002). *Inside school law, No Child Left Behind.* Alexandria, VA: Author.

National Staff Development Council. (1995). *Standards for staff development: Elementary school level.* Oxford, OH/Alexandria, VA: Author.

Neill, J. (2004). *What are the stages of group development?* Retrieved May 6, 2008 from *wilderdom.com/group/StagesGroupDevelopment.html.*

O'Connor, K. (2002). *How to grade for learning: Linking grades to standards* (2nd ed.). Glenview, IL: Pearson Professional Development.

Oczkus, L. (2003). *Reciprocal teaching at work: Strategies for improving reading comprehension.* Newark, DE: International Reading Association.

Ogle, D. (2007). *Coming together as readers.* New York: Corwin Press.

Ogle, D., & Beers, J. (2009). *Engaging the language arts: Exploring the power of language.* Boston: Allyn & Bacon.

Ohanian, Susan (2000). Goals 2000: What's in a name? *Phi Delta Kappan, 81,* 344–355.

Padak, N., & Rasinski, T. (2003). *Family literacy programs: Who benefits* (ERIC No. ED480716). Washington, DC: Eric Clearinghouse on Teacher Education.

Palinscsar, A., & Brown, A. (1986). Interactive teaching to promote independent learning from text. *The Reading Teacher, 39,* 771–777.

Peterson, K. (1995) *Teacher evaluation: A comprehensive guide to new directions and practices.* Thousand Oaks, CA: Corwin Press.

Prensky, M. (2001). Digital natives, digital immigrants. Retrieved May 9, 2008, from *www.marcprensky.com/writing/default.asp.*

Pressley, M. (2006). *Reading instruction that works: The case for balanced teaching.* New York: Guilford Press.

Rasinski, T. V. (1990). Effects of repeated reading and listening-while-reading on reading fluency. *Journal of Educational Research* 83(3), 147–150.

Reed, R. P., Jones, K. P., Walker, J. M., & Hoover-Dempsey, K. V. (2000, April). *Parents' motivations for involvement in children's education: Testing a theoretical model.* Paper presented at the annual meeting of the American Educational Research Association, New Orleans, LA.

Robb, L. (2003). *Literacy links.* Portsmouth, NH: Heinemann.

Roueche, J., & Baker, G. (1986). *Profiling excellence in America's schools.* Arlington, VA: American Association of School Administrators.

Ruddell, M. R., & Shearer, B. A. (2002). "Extraordinary," "tremendous," "exhilarating," "magnificent": Middle school at-risk students become avid word learners with the vocabulary self-collection strategy (VSS). *Journal of Adolescent & Adult Literacy, 45,* 352–363.

Schein, E. (2004). *Organizational culture and leadership* (3rd ed.). San Francisco: Jossey-Bass.

Schlechty, P. (2002). *Working on the work: An action plan for teachers, principals, and superintendents.* San Francisco: Jossey Bass.

Schloss, A. K. (2004). Fighting NCLB's "failure" label. *School Administrator, 61,* 18–21.

Senge, P. (1990). *The fifth discipline: The art and practice of the learning organization.* New York: Doubleday.

Shinkfield, A., & Stufflebeam, D. (1995). *Teacher evaluation: Guide to effective practice.* Boston: Kluwer Academic.

Silvaroli, N. (2000). *Classroom reading inventory* (11th ed.). Dubuque, IA: Wm. C. Brown.

Snow, C. (2002). *Reading for understanding: Toward an R&D program in reading comprehension* (prepared for the U.S. Department of Education's Office of Educational Research and Improvement). Santa Monica, CA: Rand Research Laboratory.

Sparks, D. (2002). *Designing powerful professional development for teachers and principals.* Oxford, OH: National Staff Development Council.

Stigler, J., & Hiebert, J. (1997). Understanding and improving classroom mathematics Instruction: An overview of the TIMSS video study. *Phi Delta Kappan, 79*(1), 14–21.

Stigler, J., & Hiebert, J. (1999). *The teaching gap, Best ideas from the world's teachers for improving education in the classroom.* New York: Free Press.

Stronge, J., & Helm, V. (1991). *Evaluating professional support personnel in education.* Newbury Park, CA: Sage.

Sulzby, E., & Teale, W. (1996). *Emergent literacy.* Mahwah, NJ: Erlbaum.

Tucker, P., Gareis, C., Stronge, J., & Beers, C. (2000, April). *How effective are portfolios in teacher evaluation?* Paper presented at the annual conference of Association for Supervision and Curriculum Development, New Orleans, LA.

Tucker, P., & Stronge, J. (2005). *Linking teacher evaluation and student learning.* Alexandria, VA: Association for Supervision and Curriculum Development.

Tuckman, B. (1965). Developmental sequence in small groups. *Psychology Bulletin, 63,* 364–399.

Tuckman, B. (2001). *Group Facilitation: A Research and Application Journal, 63,* 384–399.

Valencia, S., Hiebert, E., & Afflerbach, P. (Eds.). (1994). *Authentic reading assessment: Practices and possibilities.* Newark, DE: International Reading Association.

Valencia, S., & Place, N. (1994). Literacy porfolios for teaching, learning, and accountability: The Bellevue Literacy Assessment Project. In S. Valencia, E. Hiebert, & P. Afflerbach (Eds.), *Authentic reading assessment: Practices and possibilities.* Newark, DE: International Reading Association.

Virginia Board of Education (2003). Revised English standards of learning curriculum framework, grade 3. Richmond, VA: Virginia Department of Education.

Virginia Department of Education. (2009). *Virginia implements No Child Left Behind.* Richmond: Board of Education. Retrieved from *www.doe.virginia.gov/VDOE/ncib/.*

Vogt, M., & Shearer, B. (2007). *Reading specialists and literacy coaches in the real world.* Boston: Pearson.

Woods, M., & Moe, A. (2003). *Analytic reading inventory* (7th ed.). Upper Saddle River, NJ: Pearson Education.

INDEX

P

R

T

V

W